Rodney Eivers: Didiman

RODNEY EIVERS

Didiman

Copyright © Rodney Eivers 2023

The Author has asserted their rights under the Copyright Act 1968 (the Act) to be identified as the author of this work.

All rights reserved. No part of this publication may be reproduced, stored in a retrieval system, or transmitted in any form or by any means, electronic, mechanical, photocopying, recording or otherwise, without the prior written permission of the author. Any person who does any unauthorised act in relation to this publication may be liable to criminal prosecution and civil claims for damages.

The Australian Copyright Act 1968 (the Act) allows a maximum of one chapter or ten per cent of this book, whichever is the greater, to be photocopied for educational purposes by an educational institution holding a statutory education licence provided that the educational institution (or body that administers it) has given a remuneration notice to the Copyright Agency (Australia) under the Act.

Format and Typesetting: Clark & Mackay
Cover Design: Clark & Mackay

Self-Published by Rodney Eivers with assistance by Clark & Mackay

Proudly printed in Australian by Clark & Mackay

Rodney Eivers
Didiman
Eastern Highlands, Papua New Guinea
1955–1957

Rodney Eivers – 19 years old

Rodney Eivers, Didiman
Papua New Guinea, 1955–1957

Observations and reflections on a people's transition from a
stone-age culture to a Western economy,
through commercial agriculture.
The lived experience of a young Australian agricultural extension
adviser in the Eastern Highlands province of Papua New Guinea.

Contents

Chapter One: Introduction 1
Chapter Two: Some History and Geography 7
Chapter Three: To Papua New Guinea 15
Chapter Four: Life at Goroka 33
Chapter Five: The Job 49
Chapter Six: On Patrol 61
Chapter Seven: The Land 69
Chapter Eight: The Villagers 89
Chapter Nine: Interracial Coupling 123
Chapter Ten: Patrol Facilities 131
Chapter Eleven: The Job 143
Chapter Twelve: Health and Census 155
Chapter Thirteen: Personal Development 165
Chapter Fourteen: Supplementary Notes 173

Terminology 177
References 181

CHAPTER ONE

Introduction

Function of This Book

This book is not designed to give an overall picture of the place of the *Didiman in* Papua New Guinea in the years 1955–1957, or even of the Eastern Highlands, which was the location of my first posting as an agricultural adviser during that period. A detailed cover of the post-war application of official policies has been given by Kim Godbold in a thesis for the Queensland University of Technology.

She introduces her study:

> *Historically, the development philosophy for the two Territories of Papua and New Guinea (known as TPNG, formerly two territories, Papua and New Guinea) was equated with economic development, with a focus on agricultural development. To achieve the modification, or complete change in indigenous farming systems the Australian Government's Department of External Territories adopted and utilised a programme based on agricultural extension.*

The person on the ground appointed to provide this transformation was the *Didiman*. For the period 1955–1975, one of those officers was Rodney Eivers. This tale relates my experiences during the initial term of that role, the period of 1955–1957 spent largely in the Eastern Highlands District (now Province) of Papua New Guinea.

It is not an objective academic study. Its purpose is to provide a storage and display device and access to the public for my small number of about 50 photographs that survived 65 years of poor care and loss in transit by sea voyage via Hong Kong from PNG to Australia. Most were of colour slides that were originally of fuzzy quality or infected with mould. They are, however, the only photographic record I have of what was a very significant couple of years of my life.

Some pictures from other sources (acknowledged at the bottom of a picture) fill in some gaps or enlarge on matters not otherwise illustrated. By extensively 'annotating' individual pictures, I have used this as a device to describe some features that characterised this period of my lifetime career.

Themes

You may find several themes running through these pages.

1. One would be the sheer privilege I had of experiencing the interface of a stone-age lifestyle with the western European culture as late as the twentieth century. This was a rare opportunity for my generation, and the possibility of it being repeated anywhere else on Earth becomes more and more remote. The modern world swamps whatever indigenous cultures may have survived beyond the 19th century. A very visible demonstration of this cultural interface was the retention and display by Papua New Guinea highlands people, for this brief period of a few years, of simple but decorative day-to-day attire. Also displayed – especially in the case of women, as with the pre-European occupation for Australian aborigines – was their comfort in their near-nakedness. Less obvious and less touched on here

are the underlying deeper ceremonial and religious thought patterns, many of which will no doubt continue to influence thinking and behaviour of Papua New Guineans for many years to come. This desire for separate identity is surfacing among many indigenous people worldwide whose unique cultural arts and customs have been displaced by the dominating European culture through imposition or adoption.

2. The satisfaction that the invasion of Papua New Guinea highlands by Europeans, specifically Australians, had occurred without the violence and inhumanity, which had so evidently been part of the occupation of Australia and other preliterate cultures by people from overseas.

3. The recognition of how, in contrast to so many other societies worldwide, the highlanders had remarkably developed a land management and agriculture tradition for over thousands of years in tune with the natural environment and adaptable enough to survive the degradation that led to the demise of other cultures. Coupled with this and despite commitment to traditional practices, we have a people showing the willingness to try out new approaches, such as cash cropping, which was a major departure from their traditions of self-sustaining gardening.

4. The experience of young Australian men in handling the clash of cultures in a way which, on the whole, was accepted and even welcomed by the local inhabitants.

5. Some personally significant experiences in human relationships and the religious faith journey of a young man, perhaps naïve in his youthfulness, but with an enquiring mind and a basic nature of goodwill to all.

Why Papua New Guinea?

How did I end up on Papua New Guinea soon after my 19th birthday? To explain that, let me give a brief summary of my life history up to that point.

I am glad to be alive – to have the great privilege of actually existing. Life is a tremendous gift for all of us. From a very early age, I wanted to repay that gift in some way – to leave the world a better place than when I came into it. I picked up much of this aim from my mother, Elsie Klopper.

It also happened, however, from very early on, that I had become associated with Christianity through the Methodist and Presbyterian churches and from them absorbed the principle of the Jesus Way of loving other people even so far as to love one's enemies. That was the way I wanted to go.

I took to school readily and did well academically, but at the age of 15 years, my dad told me it was about time to start getting out and making a living.

I reasoned, 'What job can I do to make the world a better place?' It seemed to me that we all have to eat to live. To provide food, you need to be a farmer. I think I may have won a scholarship, though I can't remember, but with the encouragement of my cousin Jimmy Marshall, who was a lecturer there, I enrolled at Muresk Agricultural College to learn to be a farmer.

That turned out to be the best education I have had in my whole life. With its system of one week's practice on the farm (engaging in a varied sample of farming enterprises) alternating with one week in school learning the theories behind the practice, it was as good as any training to deal with the practicalities of day-to-day living.

I finished my three years at the agricultural college, but what about the farming? I might have some knowledge, but I did not have the capital (I might mention that at the age of 15, I had already started saving up to buy a farm). I needed to find a job. My thinking led to the conclusion, 'If I can't farm myself, perhaps I can help other people to farm.'

Somebody must have pointed me in the direction of an advertisement seeking recruits to serve as agricultural advisers in the Australian controlled and administered Territory of Papua New Guinea. In due course, after requisite enquiries, documentation and interviews, I found myself a member of the Department of Agriculture, Stock and Fisheries (DASF) of the Public Service in this land that we had inherited from Britain's colonial domains or been offered in trust by the League of Nations and the United Nations Organisation. I knew virtually nothing of this part of the world.

Nevertheless, by June 1955, two months after turning 19, I was on my way to the capital, Port Moresby.

Whether I achieved my purpose or not is hard to tell. Suffice it to say that long after leaving Papua New Guinea, I learned that the people of Papua New Guinea had been farming that land for some 30,000 years, and here I was – a white, uninformed teenager – having the cheek to seek to teach them to survive through farming. Readers and the indigenous people whom I came to know and value over my 20 years off and on in Papua New Guinea will have to judge the value of any contribution I may have made to the well-being of those with whom I interacted.

CHAPTER TWO

Some History and Geography

Location and Environment

Papua New Guinea, lying just within 2 to 11 degrees south of the Equator, is the third largest island country in the world. In land area, it is almost twice the size of Britain. And yet, it is surprising indeed that it escaped for so long the land-grabbing invasions of the European powers that had shaped the political map of the world from the time Columbus sailed to America.

As one would expect, lying as it does between 2 and 11 degrees latitude south of the Equator, the country has a typical tropical climate. It is very mountainous. Its highest mountain, Mt Wilhelm at 4508 metres (twice the altitude of Koscuisko – 2230 metres), is almost within sight of Goroka. Because of this, and with a large portion of the country covered with swampland along the path of several large-flowing rivers, it meant that there is a relatively small area of arable land. This, combined with depredation from malaria, probably contributed to the small coastal populations. Compare the neighbouring Asian nations or islands like Indonesia, for instance. This isolation from migrating peoples may also have been favoured by Papua New Guinea's not being on the major recognised trade routes of South East Asia.

Consolidation as a Nation

When the European incursion did take place, this remarkably did not occur until the late 1880s. The island ended up being split between Holland in the west, Germany in the north-east and Britain in the south-east. Through the first world war, Germany lost their territory, and Britain passed control of the south-east section (Papua) to Australia. Australia was given a mandate after the first world war over German New Guinea, modified to a Trust Territory of the United Nations. Australia then administered the two Eastern territories as one entity, leading ultimately to the transition into an independent state in 1975.

In their invasion of these islands and subsequent administration of the twin territories, Australia avoided the bloody and sometimes brutal settlement of the Australian land mass, as had happened with country occupied by the aboriginal people.[1] At least this was the case after the Second World War. Early in the century, this had not been so evident. Punitive expeditions had been undertaken in Papua, notably in 1901 and 1904, for instance, to avenge the killing of LMS missionary James Chalmers.[2]

The lack of violent intrusion and open warfare during this period as far back earlier than 1930s may have had some effect in Papua New Guineans' allowing a relatively peaceful encroachment of their lands. There would, however, have been many other factors. A major one was probably that each village and language group constituted an entity in itself, with less capacity for uniting

---

[1] Henry Reynolds, Truth Telling.
[2] (PDF) A Lesson in Violence: The moral dimensions of two punitive expeditions in the Gulf of Papua, 1901 and 1904 | Dario Di Rosa – Academia.edu.

in military resistance to an invader. After the initial confrontation, the new Australian rulers probably provided a more benevolent environment than had occurred in previous European invasions, not least in the occupation of aboriginal lands in *Terra Australis*. In some cases, as noted later in the story of Gonegiri and Wasime, despite misunderstandings that did arise, some individuals may have invited Europeans to settle on the land with them.

Then, too, it is possible that the tribespeople learned to value the imposed law, which led to less fighting between themselves and to a more peaceful environment.

It is not that inter-tribal battles did still not occur, and one still hears of them today. On several occasions with the construction of the coffee nurseries, I had prisoners working for me. They had been convicted of being involved in inter-tribal fighting but were due to be released in the near future.

On another occasion high up in the mountains at the western end of the Asaro Valley, I was standing on a ridge and looking across a deep gully to a track along a neighbouring ridge. I noticed a parade of rather dejected-looking young men making their way along the track. I asked one of the nearby villagers, 'What's going on over there?'

The answer: 'They've been in a battle, which they have lost, and are now going home after the fight, feeling pretty sore about it.'

Conciliatory policies were adopted in Papua under the long management by Hubert Murray. This was followed further post-1945, when in continuing their responsibility for administering these territories, the Australian government set out on a programme of economic development. Because of the lifestyle of the people and the nature of the indigenous economy, this led, sensibly, to exploring what could be done to extend the agricultural productivity of the land. There was some hope perhaps of improving the diet and sustainability of agricultural practices. It was perhaps not well recognised early on that the people currently living in Papua New Guinea had survived well enough with their current agricultural practices for up to the 40,000 years for which some archaeologists estimate people have lived in that location.

Eastern Highlands' Exposure to Europeans

The story of the opening up of the Highlands' valleys to European exposure by miners and later the Australian administration has become a classic example of effects of 20th century European worldwide expansion on indigenous preliterate peoples. What is so surprising about it is that this intrusion occurred so late in that era of the push into lands far away from the European centres. As explained earlier, it was not until the 1880s that Germany, Britain and Holland laid claim to the island of New Guinea, despite its being so close to the populous nations of South East Asia. It is further remarkable that during the German occupation of northeast New Guinea, no effort by the ruling authorities was made to penetrate the forested mountainous mainland. It seems to have been assumed that nobody lived there.

Not until after World War One and the transferring of a mandate to the Australian government from conquered Germany did the middle of the island come to be visited by Europeans.

It was in the 1920s, when gold fever saw miners spreading out from the well-established gold provinces in Australia, that prospectors began probing into unknown territory. From a few small centres such as Port Moresby and Lae, they followed the valleys from the coast. This led them to the unexpected spread of the grassland slopes of the Asaro and Wahgi Rivers.

The earliest best known and well documented of these explorers was a party that included Leahy brothers, Michael, Jim

Some History and Geography

and Danny and others such as Michael Dwyer, Ken Spinks and John Black.

These first arrivals were amazed to find that far from being *terra nullius*, these valleys were highly populated supporting a viable sustained agriculture.

One would like to think from my observations 20–30 years later that these were relatively peaceful incursions and that the miners dealt with their gold hunger without disruption to the local people. There have, for example, been only minor claims for possession or access to occupied land of the sort that so bedevilled relationships with Australian aborigines. I had heard of the power of firearms being demonstrated to the villagers through the shooting of an occasional pig.

The picture below, presumably shows an example of the demonstration of the deadly power of firearms.

Armed Invasion – Killing of a Pig
Photo: Internet

Sadly, I have learned that fatal confrontations did occur with the miners.

It was to better control this situation that the Government in Port Moresby in the 1930s formed an expedition of officers and 250 police to get a better handle of the situation.

This process was still going on in 1955 when I arrived. The Highlands were divided into 'controlled' and 'uncontrolled' areas. There were still 'uncontrolled' localities in the Southern Highlands, adjacent to where I was working, and there was still some resistance. In 1953, two patrol officers had been killed at Telefomin, though in the Sepik District, not the Highlands.

Pax Australiana
Kiap Ian Burnett exercising one of his roles as magistrate – possibly a family dispute in this case?

I have no awareness of firearms being used by Australian officers against the inhabitants in the post-World War Two period, and I suspect that such action would have been severely frowned upon by the officers at Port Moresby headquarters. As mentioned later, the police, including on one of the *kiap* patrols I joined, were ostentatious in their display of their .303 rifles. This, to my knowledge, was more because it was part of their uniforms rather than intended to be used in armed conflict.

It has to be conceded, though, that there were armed clashes between some of the highlands villagers and the early exploratory miners as noted elsewhere in the reference to Dan Leahy, Sr.

Exposure of the Eastern Highlands

As noted above, from colonisation in 1884 to the 1920s, Europeans ignored the centre of Papua New Guinea, because they assumed that it would be rugged, mountainous and sparsely populated. A few missionary and prospecting parties reached the edge of the highlands in the late 1920s. In 1933, Michael and Daniel Leahy flew over the Chimbu and Waghi valleys and reported vast areas of fertile, densely populated land. Extensive Administration patrols into the highlands were led by the Leahy brothers and James Taylor in 1933 and Taylor and Black in 1938. Further exploration parties were sent in during the second half of the 1930s, but it was not until the 1950s that the Administration was confident that all people in the highlands had been brought within its cover. Thus, this consolidation of what was being referred to as 'uncontrolled territory' took place over the decade that I was there, and I was familiar with several of the patrol officers involved in this process.

I met, briefly, some of these 'pioneers' who had established agricultural ventures. They included Jim and Michael Leahy and Jim Taylor but not the third Leahy brother Danny. Dan Leahy (senior) became a well-known identity with his farming at Korgua in the Western Highlands.

Dan Leahy had several local wives, one of whom outlived him. He had ten children, all of whom were well cared for and educated in Australia. He was 'reluctant to talk of his early days in New Guinea, because he worried for his children, if it were known that he and others had shot and killed warriors in armed clashes. He, nevertheless, maintained that the violence had been unavoidable.'

An enquiry was held into some 41 killings by those early prospectors and miners, but the ruling was accepted that the actions had been in self-defence, and the charges were not followed further.

Anyway, this is where I come in.

CHAPTER THREE
To Papua New Guinea

The Start – On My Way

Having finished my excellent farm management training at Muresk Agricultural College in the wheatbelt of Western Australia and wanting to have a career in agriculture, I had no capital with which to buy and operate a farm myself. I thus sought another avenue for applying the knowledge and skill I had acquired. Somehow,

Vickers Viscount – Turboprop
Photo: Internet

perhaps from a newspaper advertisement, I came across the invitation to be an agricultural adviser in the Australian territories of Papua and New Guinea.

Following an application, some documentation and an interview, I was accepted for the job and in mid-1955, just two months after my 19th birthday, I found myself heading eastward and northward.

On reflection, I recall, somewhat to my surprise in view of later travelling during my life, that this would have been the first time I had flown in an aeroplane. That in itself would have been an experience of some note. The aircraft was very innovative for its time. This plane was a Vickers Viscount, with a turboprop, as used before the days of pure jet engines. With this transitional design, which still has niche functions in commercial aviation today, it uses the jet engine to turn a propeller rather than move forward by the thrust of its jets. Its limited range required us to make one landing for refuelling en route between Perth and Sydney. Rather strangely, perhaps, the most memorable feature for me was that it had large oval windows through which one could clearly view the passing landscape. For all the improvements in large passenger aircraft since then, I have not been in any which provided as good panoramic viewing from its windows as the Viscount. Other innovations were air pressurisation and the quietness of operation compared with piston-engined aircraft.

Because of flight schedules, I needed to spend a few days in Sydney. I was booked in at one of the best-known hotels, The Wentworth. Because accommodation was tight, I was told that, at no extra cost, I was granted the very upmarket bridal suite!

While at the hotel, I was befriended by an older man, with a European accent, who provided me with something of a guided tour, I think as far as I can recall by railway, to the Blue Mountains and south to Port Kembla.

I had received very little useful 'sex education' in my life up to this point. A few weeks before I departed Perth, my father very awkwardly had tried to warn me about the dangers to young men from prostitution and other dire sexual temptations. In later years, I have thought that in my naivety I had been very trusting of this stranger. My trust, however, was justified. He behaved always as a gentleman, and I am grateful for the way he helped me feel at ease before I set off on the next stage of my journey.

On to Port Moresby

The next leg of my journey was to Port Moresby, and I cannot remember a thing about it except that it was a different aeroplane we flew in – probably a Douglas DC4 (Skymaster), and as an international flight, a different airline, Qantas. I was boarded at one of the two hotels in the town – one could hardly call it a city at that time. A middle-aged clerk from the government offices was assigned to settle me in. In my ignorance, however, I did not listen very carefully to him in his explanation of what lay before me over the next few weeks. I do not recall being given any detailed suggestions by officers from the Department of Agriculture, Stock and Fisheries (DASF). There was no introductory training for someone so new to such a unique environment. but my liaison man informed me that my initial posting was to be to the Agricultural Experiment Station in the Kainantu District of the Eastern Highlands.

He may well have explained what I would need to do while in Port Moresby to set up my domestic arrangements while serving in the field, but clearly, I wasn't listening. The reality of my situation had not sunk in.

de Haviland Beaver
Photo: Internet

The administrative officer got me organised on to the plane (probably a Douglas DC 3 of wartime vintage), then to Lae, where I was transhipped onto a Qantas de Haviland Beaver.

Aircraft Travel

I may seem to be giving undue attention to aircraft in this story. Indeed, however, aeroplanes played a large part in life outside the cities and towns in Papua New Guinea and still do. For such a vast country and needy population, the connecting road system was very limited. Now, 60 years later, there is still no road connection between the capital city in the south, Port Moresby and the second biggest town, Lae on the North Coast. This means that travel by air is a prime need. The peoples of the Highlands' provinces were first spotted from aeroplanes in the 1930s and organisations such as the Missionary Aviation Fellowship continue to give assurance of some relief for such processes as medical evacuation when vehicular links to medical facilities are non-existent.

So, whenever I travelled outside my Highlands' districts, I needed to travel by aeroplane. Although philosophically, these days I eschew risky activities like bungee jumping and aircraft joy rides, I felt reasonably confident in my travels by air in Papua New Guinea.

There were a couple of hairy experiences. On one occasion while taking off from Mendi airstrip, one of those with mountains on either side and just the pilot and me on board, the pilot found immediately after lift-off that he could not gain the altitude that

Mendi Airstrip
Photo: Internet

would have been required to negotiate the mountain passes. After fiddling frantically with the controls and gunning the engine to no effect, the pilot, with admirable presence of mind, circled around with sufficient clearance above the ground surface to finally land safely back at the air strip. I cannot recall the reason for the difficulty but understand it had something to do with the richness of the fuel supply presumably affecting the engine speed and thus the lifting power.

The second incident to cause me some anxiety was later on in Lae. I had been befriended by a young bloke named Terry, who was learning to fly. In wanting to show off his prowess, I suppose, and to build up some flying hours, he invited me to go on a flight with him. I was not keen on the idea, but in order to provide assurance of my respect and regard for him (allowing for nervousness about his limited aviation experience), I agreed to go on the flight.

We duly drove down to the airport, where he wheeled out a small Cessna-type aeroplane. We went over to a 44-gallon (200 litres) drum of aviation fuel that he hand-pumped into the petrol tank, and in due course, we (with my heart in my mouth) were away. For this flight, Terry took me along the southern coast of the Peninsula. This strip of the coastline was one I was familiar with at ground level. It followed the line of coastal villages which, taking many days at a time, I visited on foot and boat from time to time as part of my job as an agricultural adviser, so it was good to see this part of the world from an aerial angle. I could genuinely give Terry my thanks while retaining some uneasiness until we were safely back on the ground at Lae Airport.

Kainantu and Aiyura

Returning to my first-ever flight in a small plane, the Beaver from Lae to Kainantu… From the airstrip at Kainantu, I was driven for about half an hour over the ridge that separated the two settlements to the Aiyura Highlands Agricultural Research Station. The idea was to give me some idea of the agricultural cropping of that part of the world, especially of the newly instigated coffee industry.

Highlands Agricultural Experiment Station

The Highlands Agricultural Experiment Station was established in 1936 by an Australia agriculturalist, Bill Blechin, with the aim of exploring what crops might be successfully grown in these newly discovered highlands valleys. Aub Schindler was the agronomist in charge at the time of my brief stay. Coffee was always prominent, along with other crops such as pyrethrum (an insecticide) and cinchona from the bark of which the anti-malarial quinine-derived drug is derived. An airstrip was laid down, and being at the eastern extremity of the highlands, it suffered some bombing raids from Japanese aircraft during the war.

Later, years beyond my visit, that airstrip became the base in Papua New Guinea for the Summer Institute of Linguistics, a world-wide missionary group seeking to record and preserve some of the 700–800 distinct languages said to be spoken in Papua New

Guinea. The drive behind SIL was the proselytising of Christians, but internationally, they had played down that focus, and the contribution they have made to Papua New Guinea linguistics is valuable and substantial.

One of the first four national high schools was started at Aiyura in the 1970s. On a personal note, a senior teacher at that school, Gail Edoni, became a director in our family investment company and participated in the corruption-monitoring agency Transparency International.

Start in Domestication

On arriving at the Experiment Station, I was greeted by the station manager. 'Where's all your gear?' he wanted to know. I showed him my small suitcase with clothing and travel items.

'What about food?' I drew out a packet of biscuits that I had bought to sustain me on the aeroplane flight. I waved this around.

Yes, it soon became clear that I had travelled all this way completely unprepared to establish and maintain a home with appropriate facilities for living. A packet of biscuits was not going to sustain me or furnish my dwelling place for the next couple of years! In those first few weeks, I could have starved.

Fortunately, a couple among the staff, Flora and Hugo Nitsche, sized up the situation very quickly and took me under their wing. They provided me with equipment and food to carry me over and also had me up at their place for a meal from time to time.

With their instructions and those of the officer-in-charge, Aub Schindler, I learned how to order food from the coast at Lae. It came up by aeroplane about once a week or so. The meat seemed to arrive in edible condition, despite the lack of refrigeration on the aircraft. Then to aid me in overcoming my housekeeping incompetence, I was introduced to my domestic assistant (*mankimasta* – personal servant).³ His name was Waga (wah-gah). He cooked meals, cleaned the house and did the washing and ironing – particularly the ironing. He saw it as his duty to get every crease possible out of shirts, trousers, sheets and pillowcases. His most valuable role, however, turned out to be get me started in *tok pisin* (Melanesian pidgin).

This beats walking – Waga and my government-issued BSA Bantam

In the picture, you will note the clothing worn by Waga. The loin cloth (*lap lap*) was the standard dress for local men once they had lost

---

³ Terms in Pidgin English (*tok Pisin*), the lingua franca of north-eastern New Guinea, will be shown in italics from here on. See end note for a discussion of the place of Melanesian Pidgin in verbal communication in Papua New Guinea at this time.

the traditional local attire of a small skirt of twisted fibres covering the genitals. All local staff and government workers would wear the *lap lap*. This fashion would have been brought in from Papua New Guineans living in the coastal villages and may even been brought to the country from other Pacific islands. Before Western contact there had been, of course, no fabrics such as cotton and wool. Up till then for some uses, much was made of tapa cloth, which comprises the bark of a species of mulberry bush pummelled and smoothed into sheets. The wrap around loin cloth, sometimes in sophisticated and fashionable designs, remains something of a 'national dress' for men in places such as Fiji and Tonga.

As mentioned above, it was Waga who gave me my introduction to *tok pisin*. This had to be a pretty quick learning process for me during the month or so that I was there, because the local people on the station were not conversant in English, and the European staff were all fluent in pidgin. I actually became fluent in that language. I am very interested in languages. I was introduced to French and German at high school and have done short courses in several other languages including Japanese and Indonesian. Pidgin, however, is still the only language – other than English – in which I can carry on ordinary conversation.

The quarters for my stay at Aiyura were a converted Quonset Hut, one of the many residual wartime materials of structure and usage still visible and in use in 1955, only 10 years after the war in the Pacific.[4]

---

[4] A number of ex-army jeeps had been acquired by PNG residents, (see picture later with Rev Ralph Goldhardt. Many of the airstrips including the main one at Port Moresby were surfaced by Marsden matting. This comprised strips of metal sheets with holes cut along their length (presumably for aircraft wheel grip) and were hooked together to form a metallic mat upon which wartime aircraft could safely land when the underlying soil provided no firm foundation.

Quonset Hut
Photo: Internet

Black-White Racism

In a visit to Papua New Guinea some years later my brother, Kerry, noted:[5]

> 'Port Moresby was our first port of call, but we flew on to Lae, where Rodney was waiting for us. What a shock to the system.
>
> We stepped off the plane and were totally surrounded by black people.'

Perhaps from my limited preparatory reading and perhaps from my expectations of what the job was to entail, I do not recall any comparable jolt to my expectations. This brings to mind the question of racism. I am not in any way suggesting that Kerry, in this instance, was being racist. He has had far more direct interaction with Australian Aboriginal people than I, for example, and the experience has been overwhelmingly cordial. Both of us had been brought up as children in the far south-west of Western Australia, land of the Noongar people. By then, however, the local

---

[5] My Magic Carpet Ride, p. 79.

aborigines had been completely excluded from that region of the state. I do remember as a four-year-old at Katanning, a town to the east in the wheatbelt, having an aboriginal man selling firewood pointed out to me. But beyond that, we had no association at all with aboriginal people. It is dangerous for a 'white' person to claim that she or he is not racist in relation to dark-skinned people, but I can truly say that I have not been conscious of any disparagement of people of colour. I think a lot of this came from my upbringing through Sunday school Christianity. As we used to sing:

> 'Red and yellow, black and white,
> They are precious in His sight,'

In the current international climate, this may well be considered patronising, but to our childish minds, it was genuine enough.

Furthermore, in my own case, to the extent that I thought about it all, I actually regretted that, even if not racially born 'pure' Aborigine, I did not at least have some genetic connection. I could then have a truer claim to be described as Australian. Incidentally, a DNA sampling has shown that from way back in the past, I have some African genetic inheritance.

Nowadays, by a strange twist, my inclination has turned right round. I am uneasy about the current race and cultural environment wherein people who consider themselves to be aboriginal wish to be encouraged to have an identity separate from other occupiers of this land of Australia. To me, it seems difficult not to slip into genetic (that is 'racial') criteria in specifying what constitutes first nations' identity. Perhaps race and racism are two different concepts.

It is perhaps too easy for a white, male Anglo-Saxon protestant (WASP) such as myself to claim to be non-racist. I think that in my case, however, that is genuine. I do concede, though, that there may well be found from time to time a certain sense of cultural superiority that could be interpreted as racism.

For instance, on arriving in Papua New Guinea, especially the newly administered region of the Highlands, it took me a while to get used to barefooted, illiterate men being skilled enough to drive motor cars – in this location, usually Jeeps and Landrovers. Local drivers usually from the coastal towns but in due course also from the surrounding villages were customarily occupied as drivers. This did not stop European officers from being keen to drive their government-allocated vehicles and sometimes doing so. I note from my journal that I received a message from the District Commissioner (the head of the Administration for the district) reminding me of the protocols around Government officers driving vehicles.

Mind you, in relation to the use of road vehicles, I had not had that much experience with driving until working in Goroka. I had learned to drive tractors and 3-ton trucks while at the agricultural college and for holiday farm employment but had never owned or been licenced to drive a vehicle on public roads.

My first driving licence was authorised by the local policeman, Brian Holloway. When I applied to him for a licence, he simply said, 'I saw you driving up the road the other day,' and without further ado, issued me with the appropriate signed piece of paper. Not that I would endorse young people being given such responsibility without the extensive training and testing required of applicants in Australia today.

I recall very little of my time at Aiyura. The staff there were helpful, in gently introducing me to colonial culture, while I engaged in the main purpose of getting some acquaintance with tropical agriculture and the various crops that were being trialled.

One of the features of Papua New Guinea was the presence of missionaries who were taking their versions of the Christian faith into corners of the country where even the government had not exerted control until the 1930s and beyond. Before the wars, there had been many German missionaries, especially of the Lutheran and Roman Catholic persuasion. In contrast to the underlying message of the inherent equality of people no matter what their race, gender or national orientation, I learned that some of the southern American missionaries had brought their black-white racism to their task.

This was not the case, as far as I can tell, with the one American missionary family I visited while at Aiyura. My companion and I were sitting at the table enjoying a meal. The lady of the house heard a commotion and went outside and after a while returned.

Smiling, and shaking her head, she announced with a soft, warm, southern American accent, 'Those guys!'

It seems there had been some confusing interaction with some of the villagers who had been gathered outside. What has stayed with me, though, was that with her pleasant tone, despite some exasperation, she displayed a warmth in her attitude towards the Papua New Guinea people.

This was not the only memory from this visit. Not even to this day have I tasted ice cream as delicious as the helping this woman served up to us that day. She had made it herself – the nearest ice-cream shops would have been about 200 kilometres away. The creaminess of the taste of that ice cream lingers with me still.

Another example of my incipient racism came to the surface many years later. All airline pilots in 1955 would have been Europeans. I had assumed, despite the charge sometimes, that piloting an aeroplane is little more difficult than driving a bus, that flying an aeroplane was something that only the most educated of people could qualify for. That being the case, it might well be beyond the achievement of Papua New Guineans for a number of generations to come. It came as something of a surprise then to learn some 50 years later that not only were Papua New Guineans piloting passenger planes, but at least one pilot was employed as a trainer of other pilots for one of the major airlines in the Middle East!

My non-expectation in this case arose, I think, not so much from doubting the PNG's inherent capacity for such skill and roles, as from my own association with Papua New Guineans up to that time had been mainly with those who were unschooled and illiterate.

Perhaps the rugged, weather-variable aviation conditions of Papua New Guinea provide excellent conditions for acquiring aviation skills.

But back to the general subject of black-white racism, I am sure that many of the Australians who came to live and work in Papua New Guinea brought elements of the racism, which so shames our relationship with the Aborigines since the 'invasion' of their countries. There was, for instance, in Port Moresby when I arrived, a section of Ela Beach nominated for bathing by Europeans. And although paternalism rather than racism may have been behind it, alcohol was banned for Papua New Guineans. Also, I discovered some years later that for the picture theatre at Lae, certain sections were reserved for Europeans, or 'natives' were excluded altogether.

In my experience, however, for most people in the Highlands, the very wide cultural differences were acknowledged and managed. There was little sense that the people of the country, although clearly of stone-age culture, were intellectually inferior and to be 'kept in their place.' Given the history of the Aborigines and Australian settlement, this is perhaps surprising. Perhaps policy-making Australians had learned some lessons by then.

This wisdom and perhaps the granting of independence a bit too soon rather than too late has resulted in a healthy warmth of relationship between our two peoples.

It is noteworthy that during the ceremony on 16 September 1975, marking the Independence of Papua New Guinea from Australia the leading politician, John Guise, declared:

> *'Note that we are lowering the Australian flag. We are not tearing it down.'*

As recently as 2021, perhaps in connection with the Covid-19 pandemic, a rugby game, or the intrusion of China into the Pacific, a group of Papua New Guineans being interviewed made the comment.

'We and Australians are *wantoks*' (members of the same extended family).

At the time of writing in 2022, the Australian Prime Minister, Anthony Albanese, has sought to bolster this sense of fraternity (admittedly with some eye on security tensions related to Chinese government activity in the Pacific islands) by supporting the inclusion of PNG rugby teams in the Australian Rugby League competition.

After a month of orientation and familiarisation at Aiyura, mainly to do with the crops grown or being trialled for that highlands environment, I was driven along the connecting ridge via Kainantu into the next valley through Bena Bena to Goroka, the administrative centre for the Eastern Highlands District.

In picturing the access to the Papua New Guinea Central Highlands (they were remarkably little touched by the war), you may envisage a series of consecutive valleys surrounding fast-flowing rivers beginning at Lae on the north-east coast, the second largest of the Papua New Guinea cities through to the Sepik in the far west. The valleys succeed one another in steadily increasing altitudes. First, there is the Markham valley that runs westward to the Daulo Pass, thence to the Asaro river valley and the town of Goroka. Continuing westward, you climb through Waterais Pass (not sure if that was a local name or whether there used to be a water race there, i.e., for gold prospecting) to the very mountainous and very heavily populated sub district of Chimbu.

From there, the land opens up to the broad vista of the Western Highlands district and the Wahgi Valley, where a certain amount of European plantation settlement took place in due course.

My early years' experience and therefore, this tale, were limited to Goroka and the Eastern Highlands District. I had little experience with the Wahgi Valley and the more brash and somewhat rival town of Mount Hagen, the administrative and commercial centre for the Western Highlands Province.

Although I have repeated that I felt no threat of aggression, armed or otherwise, during my perambulating of the highlands villages, I may not have felt the same confidence if I had repeated the visitations in later years. There were no guns in the hands of the local people up to the 1950s, but not long after that, some men were provided with licences for shotguns. Inter-tribal tensions continued to break out in local warfare, and in due course, the villagers used some initiative to construct their own guns.

There are now gun ownership regulations legislated in the country, but this does not seem to be the pressing issue it has been in Australia since the Port Arthur massacre by Martin Bryant. In view of the difficulties of secure storage of firearms, it is perhaps surprising that they do not feature more in inter-tribal stoushes.

CHAPTER FOUR
Life at Goroka

I resided at Goroka from about August 1955 to mid-1957 and then returned to Western Australia to undertake university studies.

Town of Goroka – 1955

The Asaro River runs between the airstrip in the middle of the picture and the range of mountains in the background. The altitude is 1600 metres. The buildings shown would probably

Administration Headquarters Goroka – 1956

have been constructed with asbestos sheeting during a post-war era, before the dangers of that mineral had been recognised. Nearly all the buildings pictured would have been occupied by Europeans, predominantly Australia government officers. Papua New Guinean employees would have lived in servants' quarters situated in the grounds of the residences or coming into town from the neighbouring villages. Note that there were no sealed roads at this time.

With my trusty manservant Waga to look after my household needs and teach me the language, I settled in well at Goroka, the equivalent of a very small Australian country town at that stage.

Goroka Airport

As might be expected with a community so dependent on connection by aircraft with the outside world, the town of Goroka was built around the air strip.

There was a swimming pool adjacent to the administrative offices, although more like a household pool than anything of near Olympic standard. As described below there were picture shows occasionally from a small amateur projector.

Main Street – Goroka

Use of some facilities depended on the availability of electric power. This was supplied by a small generator only between the hours 7.00–8.00 a.m., 12.00–12.30 p.m. and 6.00–10.30 p.m.

Beyond this, for lighting, one was dependent on hurricane lamps or the much brighter Tilley design. These have a chemically-impregnated mantle that glowed brightly when ignited with kerosene fuel supplied under pressure. These simple appliances

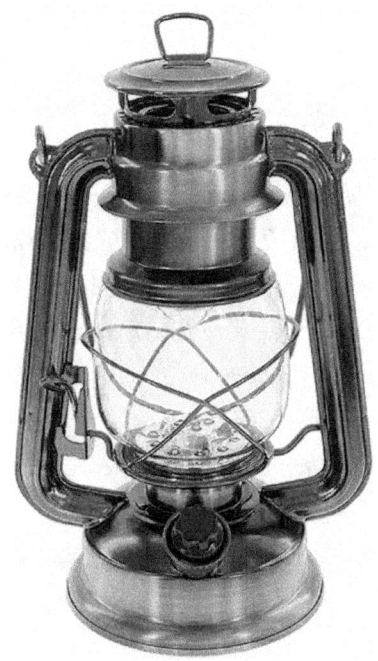 

Hurricane Lamp   'Tilley' Pressure Lamp

are not without their hazards beyond the risk of setting fire to the grass-thatched houses in which I encamped. On one occasion when cleaning the smoky glass of the hurricane lamp, the glass broke and sliced through the web of skin, separating my thumb and first finger. All these 66 years later, one can still detect a slight scar, and there is an occasional sensitive twitch from the nerve that was damaged.

One productive activity I did take up in my leisure hours was the teaching of English as a second language to the local staff. A teacher, Fred Perry, helped with ideas, materials and lesson books, and it seems that some of my assistants, particularly a tall, slim young man from the coast, Takos, took the lessons very readily.

On the whole, I was happy at Goroka, but my journal shows that I did not participate all that frequently in what socialising opportunities there might be. Often, I would babysit for my boss,

Jim Barrie, and his wife, Pam, while they went off to a dance or other social highlight. Perhaps being of a non-drinking disposition and with no unattached young women to draw me, I saw myself as being out of place in the entertainment provided by the township.

11 December 1955: Today, I had the useless feeling which usually comes when I am alone on a Sunday. It used to be the same at Muresk Agricultural College and even at home sometimes. At home, however, there is always church and Sunday school to teach, and in the afternoon, either the papers to read or a drive around the country by bike or car. At times like this, I sometimes feel like tossing the job in as there is no doubt I miss having friends, either male or female.

Single-officers' Quarters, Goroka

'Walk into Paradise'

During my time at Goroka, a somewhat unique event occurred. In conjunction with a French firm, an Australian film maker with perhaps, at that time, the best-known Australian actor, Chips Rafferty, used Goroka as their administrative base for making a film called 'Walk Into Paradise.' Viewed objectively, it was probably a pretty hammy effort both in acting and story line. It even involved an attractive French actress to play the starring female role. What it did do, however, was display the splendour of Papua New Guinea and the colour, especially, of the traditional dress of the people of this region of the country. From my own association with the people of Papua New Guinea and subsequent development of Papua New Guinea as a nation, it does, however, grate on me to hear the country referred to, in the film promotion, as 'the most primitive people on Earth.'

The traditional highlander dress, resplendent in feathers of the birds of paradise, endemic here, was on full display in the film. Although some of this apparel was worn day-to-day in the highlands villages, it was not usually highlighted to the maximum until there was a gathering of dancers (pidgin *sing sing*). I don't know to what extent the large scale of these gatherings for traditional entertainment occurred before the *pax Australiana*. Warfare between language groups seems to have been common and remains a risk now half a century later.

In the film, however, the villagers, dressed up in their dancing finery, became 'warriors' and were depicted as going on the war path with the real intent of using their spears and bows and arrows. It can be noted that the bow and arrow were inherent in their culture but mainly used for shooting birds. To me, this may have seemed pretty harmless, as there was never any aggression expressed towards me while I was in their territory. Other Europeans, however, in isolated instances, would probably have been injured by such weapons.

Filming took place mainly in the Sepik Province (then labelled 'District') in 1954 and on the Goroka airstrip, but we were told that the 'premiere' would be shown at Goroka at the time I was there.

Chips Rafferty and 'Walk into Paradise'
Photo: Internet

The townsfolk assembled in the local Administration hall with a portable screen and a home-movie type projector. Probably most of the real, serving Government officers got a bit of a laugh out of the implausibility of it all, but I guess it turned out to be a bit of fun. One side issue worth noting at a personal level is that, perhaps to give it some authenticity, the film portrayed a government officer (*kiap*) with the name Fred Kaad. This was actually the real name of the officer who acted the role. I, myself, had dealings with Fred in due course as a fellow government officer, though I was on the agricultural side of things, and he was an administrator and magistrate.

This degree of decoration would have been worn at the public gatherings called *sing sings*, not as everyday dress. The picture shows a good display of Bird of Paradise plumes and the innovation of trade store paint. The hourglass-shaped drum, the *kundu*, tapped

PNG Highlanders Dressed for Dancing.
Photo: Postcard

as shown by the hands was very common. Less common and more evident on the coast was the *garamut*. This was made of a hollowed-out tree trunk with a lengthwise open slit. It was hit with a stick and produced a booming sound. It may well have been used to send messages over a distance comparable to smoke signals, as it is claimed that American Indians among other cultures used to do. Other messages would be sent by blowing on conch shells or with gongs. Loud yodelling was also used to communicate from ridge to ridge and mountain top to mountain top.

So many times, while out on the track between villages, I would be sitting on my patrol boxes waiting for carriers. My companions, being porters from the local village we had just left would yodel a message across the valleys to let the next village know we would like some volunteer carriers to get us moving on to the next destination.

Goroka had been laid out as a town by the former District Commissioner, George Greathead, in conjunction with a local leader. Greathead left the public service and, by the time I arrived, was among the earliest of settlers to establish a coffee plantation. He had become a leading representative of the planters. Indeed, it was from these pioneering efforts that the government authorities decided that there was an opportunity to extend this agricultural initiative to smallholdings with the local people. Furthering this establishment of coffee groves by the villagers became the main function of my role as an agricultural adviser.

Churchgoing in the Highlands

The Christian faith had always drawn me from a very young age. A large part of my upbringing as a child had been in association with the belief and practice of the Christian church in its Methodist denomination. There had, however, been a break in attendance at services during my training at Muresk Agricultural College.

The Methodist church was well established in other parts of Papua New Guinea, especially in New Britain (Rabaul). Not long before I began my career in this part of the country, they had established a base in the new administrative division (still 'uncontrolled' in some parts) of the Southern Highlands. I remember meeting, once or twice, the manager of their station at Mendi, the Rev Graham Smith. He seemed to be a vigorous proponent of what the church was seeking to do. What they and I had in common was a heavy involvement in agriculture. On a subsequent occasion in Papua New Guinea, I met the late Frank Coleman, who was engaged by the mission as their agricultural adviser. When the Methodist church had a change of policy here, or perhaps a shortage of funds, Frank transferred to the government's Department of Agriculture Stock and Fisheries, my employer, although Frank did not remember me.

Some 50 years later, by coincidence, he and his wife attended the same church at Sunnybank, Queensland, as my wife Hazel and I. We shared in the same study groups and became friends for many years until his untimely death due to a brain tumour.

This is all, by the way, to note that although I had no church of my own denomination to attend, I always accepted the warm hospitality of those religious missions which operated wherever I happened to be posted. There was a Protestant church in Goroka – more on that later – and I also had some association with a group of Catholic priests in the Eastern Highlands District.

The Goldhardt family, with whom I shared some meals, eventually settled in Brisbane. Of the other members of the family, I only remember a very blonde little girl Becky. By chance I came across Ralph and Becky (now very much adult) at a gathering, probably at my children's secondary school Redeemer Lutheran College in the 1980s. To my regret, this was another case of not being recognised by someone who played some significance in my compelling past life in Papua New Guinea.

With the background of church attendance, for my social life as well as religious practice, it did not take me long to discover, and become associated with, The Goroka Protestant Chapel. The man responsible for the construction of this church building was Rev Ralph Goldhardt, who started first at St Matthew's in North Goroka and then St Paul's in town. St Paul's was then known as the 'Protestant Chapel' in which all Protestants, as well as Lutherans, went to church together.

Goroka Protestant Chapel – Goldhardt family at the top of the steps.

I attended regularly but did not get involved in the administration of the congregation to the extent I did with other churches I joined later. This may have been partly because of my youth and partly because I was not at home with the Lutheran culture that was behind the establishment of this congregation. Not that people from other denominations were discouraged; the very name of the chapel denies that. Indeed, one of my records shows that I was invited to be a 'deacon.' I think this role is that of a general dogsbody in relation to preparation and conduct of services. I don't recall, though, to what extent I was involved in carrying out that role.

There is, however, one memory that stays in my mind perhaps linked to the Lutheran background. We had a preacher who was either a replacement for Ralph Goldhardt or a visitor. He was a tall American, and it was on this occasion that I was reminded that behind Lutheranism, there is a strong historical consciousness of the tension between Protestantism and Roman Catholicism. This led to Martin Luther's separation from the universal church of that time.

This minister, in illustrating this theme, used as his hymn the very well-known tune sung at least once a year in every church I have attended, 'The Church's one foundation is Jesus, Christ, her Lord.' Presumably, these words are sung to emphasise the Protestant counter to the Catholic doctrine of elevation of the Pope and the Vatican. Now, after 66 years, every time that song is sung, it takes me back to that sermon at the Protestant Chapel in the centre of the town of Goroka. Until then, I had no idea that the hymn might be linked to the theme of the Protestant Reformation.

In later years, around 1963–1966, I had further association with the Lutheran church in Papua New Guinea. This was especially with their station at Kaiapit in the Markham Valley. These missionaries were also American. The Lutheran church was established in the Territory during the control of north-eastern New Guinea by the German government. When Australia took over control from Germany after the first world war, many of the German missionaries stayed on in Papua New Guinea. Their replacement by American personnel continued after the Second World War. Lutheran missionaries were among the first Europeans to venture into the highlands of Papua New Guinea in the 1930s. Several of these American missionaries, like the Goldhardts, settled in Australia after Papua New Guinea's Independence.

Field Marshal Sir William Slim – Australian Governor-General
Photo: Internet

Life at Goroka

Another claim to fame came during my residence at Goroka. Because of its unique place in Australian history, the highlands and its centres, Goroka and Mount Hagen, received a fair bit of attention from visiting dignitaries.

The Governor-General of Australia at that time was Sir William Slim. He had earlier gained high repute through his vocation as a military commander in both First and Second World Wars. He had also in the 1930s written some novels under the name Anthony Mills. He made his high military reputation from the Burma campaign. Then, from 1953 to 1959, he became the 13th Governor-General of Australia. I believe he may have been the last British appointee to the role before it became reserved for Australian notables.

In his role as the top nominal leader in Australia, Slim presumably fulfilled this role by visiting the Australian Trust Territory of New Guinea, including Goroka. Apparently, it was his custom to attend church services on Sundays, so despite being born into a Catholic family, his schedule took in a visit to our Protestant Chapel on a weekend when I had taken a break from my patrolling the villages.

Somehow, we regular members of the congregation, with the requisite security and administrative personnel in the background, came to be lined up and 'shook hands' with the Governor-General. I think we may have even had a brief conversation.

CHAPTER FIVE
The Job

Several of the regrets I have over my time in Papua New Guinea were that I was not better prepared for the assignment and, that in my employment, I was not involved more in policymaking in regard to agriculture advisory aims in the territory.

I had no knowledge of the country in general, let alone the highlands, when setting off from Western Australia. The only book I had read on that part of the world and its cultural environment was 'Growing up in New Guinea' by distinguished anthropologist, Margaret Mead. Her study, however, was limited to the island of Manus (see Lorengau on the map frontispiece), which had little relationship, if any, to the peoples and culture of the PNG Highlands. I envied the Patrol Officers in the Administration in that they were given a period of training at the ASOPA (Australian School of Pacific Administration) in Sydney before they took up their positions overseas. I did seek to counter some of my ignorance of preliterate cultures years later, in 1962, when I did a one-year course in anthropology at the University of Western Australia.

In relation to policymaking, maybe that was not my role. Agricultural advisory staff did have group consultations from time to time that were of value. It is possible, however, that I could have made more effort to move more into the general decision-making area rather than feeling a little bit out on the edges from my colleagues.

Anyway, for my first two years posting in the Highlands, I was there very much to do what I was told rather than to raise new ideas.

In practice, this meant the establishment of village holdings in the infant coffee-growing industry. An extensive amount of my patrolling time comprised the construction and stocking of fish ponds. There was also some attention to food gardening, which had to be balanced against my limited awareness – not so evident to me at the time – of the success of the inhabitants of these valleys and mountain sides in pursuing their own sustainable agriculture.

Nevertheless, I felt sometimes that there was some lack of balance here, seeing it was a subsistence economy, and the immediate need of the villagers was to provide sufficient food to stay alive. As alluded to above, and as I may mention elsewhere, at that time I did not sufficiently take into consideration that archaeological studies show that there have been people in the Highlands subsisting well enough agriculturally for some 30–40 thousand years.[6] This was brought home to me some 50 years later.

On the matter of the relative importance of subsistence agriculture as against cash cropping, perhaps that awareness makes the point. As will be listed later, there were quite a few introduced food crops growing well before my colleagues and I got there, but the people had survived happily with their traditional range of foodstuffs based around the carbohydrate nutrient of universally cultivated sweet potato. The rationale for our introduced concept of cash cropping could justifiably be laid on the need for economic surpluses to support education, infrastructure and welfare services. This could only be achieved through gardening for profit. Failing that, dependency on economic development had to come, as it

---

[6] Jared Dimond Chapter X Collapse.

The Job

very much has done subsequently, from other commercial activities such as mining and forestry.

Mentors and Colleagues

Very much a major part of my patrolling of the villages was carried out alone over my two years, as far as companionship with other officers went. There was a series of young men, however, who did join me either to mentor me or for me to mentor them as an introduction to this rather unique career. There are pictures of David Montgomery and David Sergeant elsewhere in this account.

Agricultural officers (Didiman) at Goroka – David Sergeant, David Montgomery and Jim Barrie.

This picture is included not so much to record the names of the staff but to note what was the standard 'uniform' for government officers at that time in Papua New Guinea. Normally, it became second nature to wear this clothing. Coming back to Brisbane after all these years, I still have the mental adjustment to make that long socks are no longer *haute couture* for men's fashion. As a result, there is quite a number of unopened packets of long socks still lingering in my clothes drawer and overdue for discard.

Jim Sharp

Not pictured is Jim Sharp. Ginger-haired Jim was the person who took me on and 'trained' me during my initial patrols. These were mainly to the Bena Bena subdistrict east of Goroka.

Recollection of Jim's role in 'instructing' goes without record except for one thing. This relates to a general experience in my life that may be touched on in these and other pages as we go on. We meet many people over a lifetime, and they may or may not have a lasting impact on us. In the recording of these and other memories, there have been people I met who made a lasting impression, but in later life when I have ventured to say 'Hullo,' they have indicated that that have no memory of ever having met me. I respond to these revelations with some chagrin. Of course, the reverse does happen occasionally when I cannot recall connection with someone who has approached me.

On the other hand, there were several of these from my time in Goroka with whom I had minimal contact but said or did something which got imprinted in my memory. Jim Sharp was one of those. He was supposed to be 'training' me. I would ask him questions: 'How long is it to the next village? What will we be doing there? Whom will we meet?' and so on.

Jim would answer, 'Well, how would I know.' This response frustrated me no end. I thought about it. Why was this so? On reflection, I decided that it was because I was not necessarily looking for a factual answer. What would have been satisfying and probably just what I was looking for was an 'opinion.' After all, Jim had more knowledge of the situation we were in, and likely to find. His giving me an opinion even when he had no 'factual' answer would have at least given me a bit of information to work on. The outcome is that since that time, 65 years ago, when someone asks me a question, I endeavour to give that person an answer, even if it is only my opinion or understanding relating to the information sought. A variation of this response at the time of writing is that when I am given a withering response to my own questions and comment, I explain, 'I am just seeking to make conversation.'

David Montgomery

David Montgomery was the officer who took over from me when I finished my first two-year term and was not posted back to Goroka. He stayed on the job until 1959. Remarkably, I did not discover until some 50 years later that he had broadcast on the ABC and written extensively about his time as a *Didiman* in the Papua New Guinea highlands. He had provided far more detail than I have memory for, although I am able to supplement my story from my daily journals. What David has done, though, is provide a reference to what we actually did on the job. It is a remarkable coincidence that this full description of a highlands agricultural adviser's job should be provided by one I mentored. He thus covers so much of my own experience that there is no need to repeat much of it in these pages.

For this and other reasons, my tale is more anecdotal of my personal reactions and even lifelong learnings as demonstrated in the episode with Jim Sharp and his reply to my questions.

David has even provided a very extensive website account:

https://pngaa.org/article/didimans-diary-11-by-david-montgomery/

Prospectors, Planters and Descendants

As you will note from the bulk of this tale, my main role was to provide agricultural advice and moral support to the smallholder villagers. In the introductory history of the 'opening up' of the Eastern Highlands, I referred among others to the Leahy brothers and others as gold prospectors.

Jim Taylor

The unauthorised expeditions stimulated the government administration to take more interest in this 'uncontrolled' territory, and Jim Taylor was leader of the police team in late-1938 that set out to bring some administrative control and legal order for the newly contacted populace.

Kiap Jim Taylor entering the Highlands.
Painting by Papua New Guinean artist Simon Gende

The Job

These two groups of interlopers and the means of their entry have been granted legendary status in the history of Papua New Guinea. As soon as it was made available by the Government, a number of these earliest Australian visitors settled in the Eastern Highlands, taking up land gazetted by the Territory Administration for agricultural or grazing purposes. As mentioned elsewhere, I briefly met several of them, including Jim Leahy and Jim Taylor, together with former District Commissioner George Greathead. They were in the process of establishing the new crop of coffee. With good reason, they saw the Eastern Highlands as having comparable climatic condition to the internationally known Blue Mountain coffee plantings in colonial Kenya. One of my first activities at Goroka was to accompany my boss Jim Barrie to the plantations of these three farmers when they discussed some of the hiccups they were having with getting the coffee plantings going on a commercial scale. My journal, from visits to their properties, reports that their planting skills and knowledge at that stage were somewhat limited.

I don't know whether the DASF recognised that for these former prospectors and public servants, their knowledge of coffee planting needed some encouragement. During my time there, however, there took place an initiative of the local Planters Association, with the Department of Agriculture, to finance and organise a visit to the region by Y. Baron Goto of Hawaii. He was considered to be something of an expert in the field at that time.

Some of these early settlers married local women, and there followed several dynasties from these unions. In the case of Jim Taylor, one outcome of this was his daughter Margaret (Meg) Taylor.

Dame Meg Taylor

Honoured currently as Dame Meg Taylor, she was one of the two daughters of Jim Taylor and his wife Yerima. She became a prominent Papua New Guinea lawyer and was Ambassador of Papua New Guinea to the United States, Mexico and Canada in Washington DC during 1989–1994. In 2014, she was appointed as Secretary General of the Pacific Islands Forum. Her term with the Forum expired in May 2021 at a time of some turbulence in that organisation.

Some Local Produce

Sir Daniel Leahy

One day, as a break from the long and sometimes wearying walks of my agricultural patrolling, I stopped to take a breather on a handy rock at a beautiful little spot in the shade. It was on the bank of brook at a point in the main east-west (still unsealed) road. There was a ford for vehicles at this point where the water ran over the road. A Land Rover came up the road. The vehicle, towing a trailer of goods, crossed the ford, then pulled up. When it was parked, a young man of about my own age hopped out of the vehicle and came to join me. He offered me a pineapple, a fruit that I was not accustomed to in my life in Western Australia. As something of one of those irrelevant experiences that persist in the memory, I recall a lot of discomfort, because the acidity of the pineapple made my mouth sting.

The man offering me this temporary companionship introduced himself as Danny Leahy. I learned that he was the nephew of one of the famous Leahy brothers, Michael, who ran a

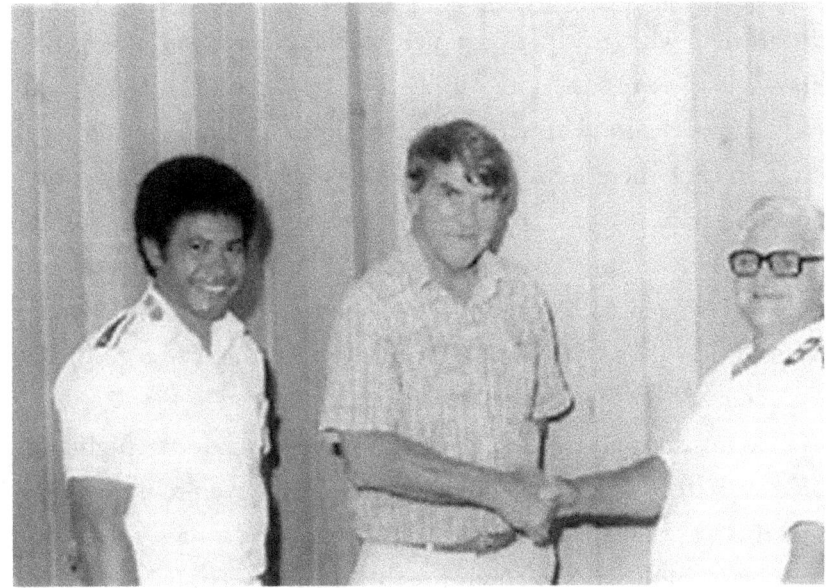

Daniel Leahy (Centre)

cattle farm at Zenag south-west of Goroka. Dan had followed his uncle to Goroka and begun simple 'trading' with the local people. This was not comparable with the exchanging of goods characterising the activity of traders and native peoples in America. It was closer to basic retailing of western style food and clothing. He was continuing to set up small grass-thatched 'trade' stores accessible to the villagers throughout the surrounding Eastern and Western Highlands at the time of our chin wag.

Subsequent to our meeting at the roadside, he expanded his commercial interests to the extent that by 1994, after combining with Steamships Trading Company, his firm as 'Collins and Leahy' became probably the largest retailing organisation in the country. He had many interests in the community well beyond Papua New Guinea Independence in 1975 and was in due course awarded a knighthood.

Job Performance

I have no reason to think that my public service employers were dissatisfied with my performance in the role. I did not get to know closely my superiors – Bill Conroy, Director of DASF, and Jack Lamrock, in charge of the extension (smallholder advisory) division. For these first two years, I was well aware of my junior position. There was some comment by headquarters' staff, favourable I assume, that I had spent much more of my time in the field on patrol to the villages, when compared with that of other officers. I seemed to have created something of a record in the extent of that village patrolling.

To my disappointment, I was not posted back to the highlands on return from my first biennial leave and was given to understand that this was to widen my experience beyond the somewhat unique advisory region of that environment. Thus, the transfer was not related to the effectiveness of my employment in that region.

It would be remiss of me, however, to omit the record of an episode that did severely blot my copybook.

Beside their advisory role, agricultural staff had the responsibility to monitor and apply plant and animal quarantine statutory regulations. I admit to complete naivety for those first few years about the rules I was to apply. Thus, on one occasion, one of the local European planters – Ian Downs (another former District Commissioner) – came into the agricultural office to approve the sending of a live pot-plant to Australia. I looked it over, and it seemed healthy enough, so I signed the appropriate authorisation, and the applicant duly posted it off to its Australian destination.

When it got to its port of entry to Australia, however, the quarantine authorities jumped on it straight away and notified their counterparts in Papua New Guinea. I then got a rocket from the Director of the Department, Frank Henderson, in Port Moresby critical of my major faux pas. Of course, my local boss Jim Barrie also bore the brunt of some of this.

I had committed the serious misdemeanour, from the Australian authorities' point of view, of authorising the entry of unsterilised soil into that country – the soil in the pot that held the plant!

I felt duly contrite, and I must emphasise here my full ongoing support of the well-known strong agricultural quarantine stance taken by Australia.

CHAPTER SIX

On Patrol

While based in Goroka, I spent close to most of my time out in the villages in the mountains surrounding the town – on patrol, you might say. The meaning of the word 'patrol' comes from going the rounds, usually in a military sense. Well, this was certainly in no military sense, but going the rounds applies pretty well. And 'going the rounds' at this time meant going by foot. Unless they happened to have the few arterial roads pass close by, the great majority of all the villages could only be reached by foot. It is one of the ironies of the development of communication in Papua New Guinea that for many parts of the country – this may well still apply to some parts – the next step from travelling by foot was to travel by that high-tech facility, the aeroplane.

The 'patrolling' requiring walking, and camping seemed the natural way to reach the people, and I thought there was nothing exceptional about it. I learnt in due course, however, that it had come to the attention of my superiors in the Department of Agriculture, Stock and Fisheries. I learned that, for that period, I had earned some acknowledgement as the field officer spending the largest proportion of his working time out in the villages 'on patrol.' This information came apparently from the records provided through my applying for the camping allowance made available to officers working in the bush environment.

Road and Track

A connector road had been built linking the three districts of Morobe (administrative centre, Lae), Eastern Highlands (Goroka) and Western Highlands (Mount Hagen), but there was not much else for use by the villagers. Roads were ongoing objects of construction, supervised by the *kiaps*. They were built with hand labour, and none were sealed.

Bena Bena Roadworks – 1956
A shady rest from his labours.
The pidgin term is *kisim win* (get your breath back).

This labourer was engaged in building a road, and the picture showing a spade illustrates the limitations of the tools and implements available and used to build roads in this part of the country at the time. In 1955, the road network was being lengthened extensively. It was often in mountainous terrain, and all of it was carried out with willing manual labour using tools no larger than spades and crow bars. Land slippage was always a risk because of the very weathered nature of the red underlying soil on the steep slopes. On the other hand, there was very little underlying rock, and this made digging and moving the soil a lot easier. Note also the traditional everyday dress of the man in the picture even when occupied with such a task.

Rev Ralph Goldhardt of the Lutheran Mission, Asaroka.

Agricultural patrol assistants and camping gear heading for the end of the vehicular road. Note the red underlying road surface of weathered rock topped with river gravel to minimise rut formation.

Ralph Goldhardt with wartime disposals Jeep and Rodney Eivers on BSA Bantam motor bike

In the background is a good clump of the very common wild canegrass (in pidgin *pit pit*). This native plant was very widely used in Papua New Guinea. All buildings would comprise plaited sheets of this *pit pit* topped off with a thatch of *kunai* grass (*Imperata spp*). Of special significance to Australians is that this grass, generically *Sacchurum robustum*, was the forerunner of sugar cane. Scientists say that the sweeter specimens were identified by the chewer, then selected and cultivated to produce the *S. officinarum*. It is now grown in plantations all over the world but originated in Papua New Guinea. The development of the canefields of Eastern Australia was aided by research and breeding of cane varieties from Papua New Guinea. There are many home-bred varieties of sugar cane in village gardens, and I was frequently given a sample to chew on and be refreshed with in my perambulations around the countryside.

At the age of 19 years, I had never owned a vehicle and did not have a driving licence. This is not to say that I had no driving

Transport at last
Me and my BSA Bantam.

experience. I had freely driven tractors at the agricultural college. At one of my holiday farm-work experience places in the West Australian wheat belt, I learned how to 'double declutch' on a 3-ton farm truck with an old-style gearbox. I was quite proud of myself for that!

Muresk College had received one of the first Ferguson tractors to be brought to Western Australia.

Up till about the end of the Second World War, farm tractors did their job by passively dragging farm implements, such as ploughs, behind them. Irish engineer Harry Ferguson, however, designed a system using hydraulics incorporated in the tractor to manipulate the implement in various ways. He won a major patent case against the Ford company in the United States. Many years later, I was chuffed when touring in Ireland and unintentionally happened to visit an old school in a remote village. It was recorded there that this was the very school where Harry Ferguson began his education.

My final college holidays job while at Muresk was to use a Fordson tractor with dozer blade to level the Aussie Rules football ground. So my first driving licence was granted by a somewhat offhand process at Goroka to allow me to drive the official Land Rover, whenever I was allowed access to it. For my specific use in village-patrolling duties, however, I was allocated this 175 cc motorbike – green and cream in colour from the BSA (Birmingham Small Arms) factory.

This was all very nice, but there were not many vehicular roads to use it on, especially when you rose up in altitude into the mountains flanking the Asaro valley. Furthermore, all roads were unsealed.

The soil was a sticky red clay. Thus, when riding this machine, a great deal of my time after one of the frequent showers of rain was spent stopping at the roadside to remove the clay that was clogging up the wheels and had brought my conveyance to a halt. Very frustrating and a bit worrying if I could not get going again by nightfall.

Tuesday 18th September 1956: I have had a great deal of trouble with the motor bike. It was raining that afternoon and I had a greasy time getting down to the mission. When I started off home, I found that I couldn't move after a few hundred yards due to the wheel becoming clogged up with mud. I revved and I roared but couldn't get it to budge. I ended up dragging it to a firm, strong surface and cleaning out some of the mud. I managed to start and make another 600 yards but an ungravelled stretch stopped me again. I abandoned the bike.

David Montgomery – Snack Time.
Pit pit cane in the background with some of the villagers for company

Thirsty?
Refreshment from a roadside spring (not clearly visible). Note the youth's decorative dress.

CHAPTER SEVEN
The Land

Land Management

To the Australian outsider familiar with visions of the wartime Kokoda Track, it is easy to assume that Papua New Guinea is a land covered with rain forest – jungle. This would certainly be mostly true except for those large swamp areas dominated by sago palms and other vegetation with wet feet in the west of the country. In the

Bena Bena Landscape

populated highlands, however, much of the forest has disappeared, presumably through repeated firing of the vegetation and agricultural overuse. The burning would accompany increased cultivation and shorter bush-fallow periods as the population increased, leading to loss of soil fertility. The hills and ridges become seas of grass – *kunai* in Pidgin. The main species of these grasses is *Imperata sp.* It is known as Blady Grass in Australia.

The tracks between villages traversed these grass-covered ridges. In the photograph, a typical walking track can be seen rising from the bottom right to the top left of the picture. The absence of trees could make conditions pretty warm as the day wore on, but on the whole, at these altitudes, the days were as pleasant as in springtime in South-East Queensland or South-Western Australia

This is a poor photograph but again illustrates faintly the path rising from left to right up the grassy slope. There is also the picture of some village huts – possible linked to cultivated areas – built in a valley rather than the usual practice of on a ridge. There is some attempt to restore the forest to these degraded grassy areas. Part of my job, however, in the mid 1950s was not so much a matter of restoring the forests but of utilising parcels of land for forestry plantations. Teak was introduced to Papua New Guinea by the Germans in the early 1900s, and some 3,500 ha of plantations were subsequently established. Teak timber is particularly valued for its durability and its water resistance, and the fact that imported Papua New Guinea teak is now advertised for sale in Australia indicates that those early plantations succeeded to some degree. As a plantation crop, these imports may do something to ameliorate the damage being dealt out to Papua New Guinea forests through intense exploitation in recent decades of the extensive old-growth forests.

Land slip

Grassland

Taken clearly from a high altitude (possibly 2,000 metres) after perhaps a weary day's walking. One sees the grasslands merging into the mountain forests. The pale patch towards the bottom right of the picture may be a land slip. These are also common in this geologically young environment with deeply weathered soils. It is possible, however, that this 'scar' reveals a steeply sloping mountain side that has been brought into cropping. This also was not unusual, as villagers sought, through their bush-fallow rotation, to bring into cultivation the increasingly rarer patches of forest that had been resting for some years.

Grassland Village

One sees a scattering of the classic circular grass-thatched houses. The ceilings were low, probably to retain heat in the cold sub-alpine climate. The 'square' fenced patches above the houses would be gardens, mainly of sweet potato – *kau kau*.

The end result of the closer cultivation, and perhaps some uncontrolled burning, is these extensive covered slopes. Occasionally, as in this instance, a tall, isolated forest tree, a hoop pine, may be allowed to survive. The example shown is a species of the Araucaria genus of which well-known examples in Australia are the hoop pine, bunya and Norfolk Island pines. As in Queensland, the hoop pine is the most common of the group. Another well-known species in Papua New Guinea is the klinki pine. With the hoop

Remnant Hoop pine in Residual Grassland (Kunai) – Bena Bena

pine, these latter two very tall subtropical forest timbers provided the raw material for the major plywood manufacturing plant at Bulolo in the Morobe Province.

In the following picture "Lone Pines" these remnant forest trees on the skyline are possibly the klinki pine from the Araucaria family. This species is the tallest (up to 90 metres high and 3 metres diameter) of that family and familiar in the Papua New Guinea highlands. Like the hoop pine in Queensland, they rise to well above the general canopy of the tropical forest. As a species, however, they are at risk. As this and other pictures would attest, shifting agricultural cultivation has not been kind to them. As an excellent plywood timber, they also suffer from commercial exploitation. There has been some counter to this with the establishment of plantations to supply the Bulolo plywood mill.

Lone Pines

'Ow! That hurt.'
An unwelcome encounter with the prickly leaves of the indigenous Klinki Pine

The Land

Carrier Team

Carriers were recruited, often by yodelling calls, usually willingly but sometimes with long waiting periods, as one crossed the tribal boundary of one group into the next.

Distances between villages could be rather long. My journal records at least one walk of 20 miles (32 km), and there was a series of walks over several days ranging from 5 hours to 9 hours in duration. Once or twice, there were distances of 32 km covered in one day.

Ever Upward – Patrol Carriers Scaling the Ridge – Bena Bena

One could be weary and footsore after efforts such as these in often mountainous country. Some of the villages were located at, or above, the 'moss line' (2400 metres). Particularly at the western end of the Eastern Highlands, reaching them could reveal some breathtaking views. I recall one especially long and demanding day passing through the mountain forests near Chuave. Reaching the ridge at the summit, we broke into the clearing in which the village of Koko was sited. There, into the far distance, one experienced the awe-inspiring sight of broken country and striking land formations dominated by the near-perpendicular face of Mt Elimbari in the Simbu subdistrict. It was a view that it would be hard to rival anywhere.

Mt Elimbari featured on a postage stamp.
Photo: Internet

I have to say that although it could warm up in the middle of the day, while traversing the grassy patches, the climate was mild enough to minimise the discomfort from the degree of cold one would find at these altitudes in other parts of the world. The forest tracks, apart from the sticky ground underfoot and despite the popular depictions of the Kokoda Track, elsewhere, sometimes were pleasant to traverse.

Suspension foot bridges of cane or rope had been constructed when the rivers were too full and fast-flowing to wade across. Not that there was no wading, up or down stream. In these instances, one had to cope with the instability of smooth rocks rolling under foot, making the floor of the rivers tricky to navigate.

One of the steeper river banks

The Land

The Track

Believe it or not, this was the nature of the track between some of the villages of the Asaro Valley or for access to the gardens. Agricultural Assistant Officer David Sergeant having a bit of a struggle there. Being sloping grassland, there was no advantage of the forested country of having vines and tree roots to provide a grip.

Wading the stream

Kauri Pine
Note the *Cordyline 'dress'* and the rod of sugar cane.

Forest and Stream

Here, by contrast, is a sample of the old-growth forest that survives once one rises from the floor of the major valleys to the mountainous ridges, where the original vegetation remains dominant. This massive tree is one of the two kauris (*Agathis* spp.) endemic to Papua New Guinea. Other kauris are well-known components of native forests in New Zealand and Australia. Because of the large girth of individual trees and the absence of knots, kauri can be a valuable construction and furniture timber.

The Land

One More River to Cross
The occasional rope bridge over a major river.

Observable in this photograph are the carriers engaged with their patrol boxes slung on poles. The boxes contained the camping equipment, food and other resources needed while on patrol. They were made of galvanised steel with strong metal loops at each end through which poles could be inserted to be borne on the shoulders of the carriers.

Some hazardous turbulence

The carriers were usually willing enough. They were paid something that would be far from award wages by today's standards. It was usually money but could be various goods and in earlier days scarce items such as household salt and mother-of-pearl shell. Tobacco was also a tradeable item. It was sold and used in the form of twist tobacco. This comprised compressed leaves of tobacco heavily impregnated with molasses.

In usage, the dark-coloured 'twist' is broken into small pieces and wrapped in newspaper or some broad leaf such as *tanget*.

30 January 1956

A rather funny incident happened at about a quarter past ten last night. I was lying in bed in the haus kiap thinking of a short article written in the Countryman magazine which I had been reading at dinnertime. I suddenly woke up to the thought that I'd like to keep the particular article. I then remembered that I had given it to Yauho to use for rolling his cigarettes. I quickly yelled out (nearly everyone was asleep by now) for Yauho. The result was I had men and boys from all over the place, including the policeman, standing at my window wondering what was wrong. Of the three sheets of newspaper I had given him, Yauho still hadn't used one. I was very happy to find that with this one, he still retained the article I wanted. A cigarette had already been made out of the first two paragraphs. The more important part was still there, so I was able to tear it out and give Yauho the rest of the paper. I then sent myself and everyone else back to bed!

I have been unable to establish whether tobacco grew naturally and was cultivated in Papua New Guinea before the European arrival, but I would think it was a common practice in *bipotaim* (before time – from the beginning). Perhaps there was some other local plant used rather than the *Nicotania* sp. of common tobacco.

The Land

Today, Papua New Guinea is among the top ten countries in the world in terms of tobacco consumption – around 40% of the population consumes tobacco. It is an important development challenge, imposing a significant burden to households, particularly poor households.

Smoko!

In my visits to the villagers of the Eastern Highlands, I would come across young and old men smoking pipes. These seemed to be simple short tubes of bamboo, and they took pride in demonstrating how they would puff away. Whether it was traditional or something introduced in German times from the coast, I don't know, but tobacco was certainly popular in 1955. Indeed, there were efforts made to encourage plantings of tobacco, and much income has been earned by villagers in a number of districts. As in the Western world, because of the serious health issues, authorities are now taking steps through publicity and legislation to rein in the practice.

Photo: R Eivers 1963
Tobacco crop inspection – Markham Valley

The other common 'drug' throughout the coastal altitudes of Papua New Guinea is betel nut. The betel nut palm and ancillary pepper vine do not readily grow at the highlands altitudes, but the chewing of this palm product has become increasingly universal with the influx of people from the coast.

Back to Carriers

My local agricultural assistants had to be relied on to recruit carriers. There was a change of team every time we passed from the territory of one tribal group to another. If I ever sensed any major strain in my life of walkabouts from village to village, it was over the recruitment of carriers. It was a frequent occurrence for me to spend some hours sitting on the patrol boxes waiting for the next batch of men – and occasionally women – to move all the accompanying gear. One would listen to the men in their decorative headdresses and decorations yodelling backwards and forwards across the valleys as they sought to let villagers know of our presence and that we would like some help. It is not that the villagers were resentful about the practice. They accepted this responsibility perhaps as being just the Australian administrative way. I had the perception, also, that in most instances, they actually liked us to visit their villages.

I found this phenomenon of a warm welcome by country people to visitors from the city when employed in another area of operation later on. When based at Port Moresby headquarters, although in rank not much above lowly clerk, I seemed to have some extra authority when greeted by people in outlying town and centres. Just the fact of coming from the capital city somehow gave an additional aura of status. I suspect this interaction occurs in many fields, both government and private. Perhaps there is also this element in the enthusiasm with which members of royalty are made to feel at home in villages, towns and countries remote from the centre.

My carriers were usually young to middle-aged men, but girls and women would be called on and ably provided the service if the men were not available.

As contact with the coastal districts continued to grow in the 1950s, many of the young men were absent. They travelled to the lowland centres for employment. It has been fortunate for Papua New Guinea that in contrast to other developing countries, especially in Africa, there have not been strong regional alignments. I understand that the Papua vs (north-east) New Guinea differentiation, which used to be evident, tended to be played down as national consciousness grew. There was, years later, the secessionist 'war' in Bougainville, but this had commercial and administrative underpinnings rather than that of tribal identity.

The young men from the Eastern Highlands who did find employment away from home were for a while known collectively as 'Chimbu,' although the Chimbu District (now Simbu Province) was the origin of only some of the highlanders.

I must note here that although the dependence on local carriers led to some frustrations in liaison and communication, I was blessed in that I did not have to carry anything myself. This, of course, is in contrast to those who engage in recreational 'backpacking.' Thus, my excursions from village to village for as long as eight hours could sometimes be wearisome but otherwise pleasant and not exhausting.

Kiap Ian Burnett and Police Officer

There are many rivers and streams throughout Papua New Guinea. The Highlands are no exception to this. One of my journal entries records the crossing of the same river five times during one expedition. Far from the scene above showing an example of colonial oppression, it depicts what was a common experience. The Australian officers, as you can see, wore shoes or boots and long socks. It would become tiresome to have to take off one's shoes every time there was a creek to be crossed. When it was necessary to get to the other side without getting wet, our Papua New Guinean staff would insist that we were given a lift as you see in this photograph. Perhaps they took some pride in this as a display of their strength and perhaps a demonstration that when it comes to traversing this country, bare feet rather than shoes have some advantage. Not that it was always a dependably stable ride. Because of the instability of the rounded rocks on the bed of the stream underfoot, I ended up tipped into the water on one or two occasions.

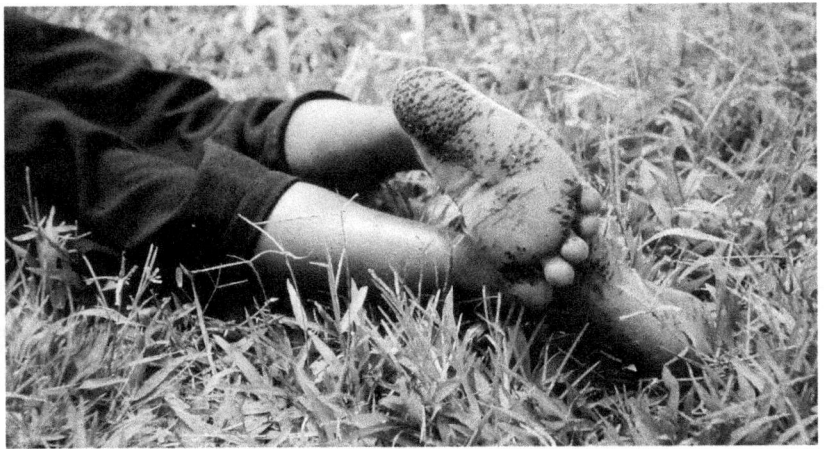

Bare Feet Have their Penalties

Despite the comfort and better grip experienced by the highlanders, with their customary bare feet when walking, the callused regeneration of the soles of these feet of one of our staff shows the damage that can occur.

CHAPTER EIGHT
The Villagers

Greetings

Coffee and Teak Party

Why the calling for this spectacular group photograph was organised for my benefit, I don't recall. Clearly, however, I was being welcomed, and it looks as if the cheerful young people are about to transplant their coffee or teak timber seedlings. There are many young women in the working party with an impressive display of their *kina* (pearl shell neck plates). *Tanget* bushes and a mountain provide an ever-present background.

It may be that in hindsight I tend to paint a picture that is rosier than it actually was. The impression remains, however, that I was generally given a warm and indeed often enthusiastic reception. There were times when villagers lined up along the central village passageway to call out their '*moning!*' (Good morning) or '*apinun*' (Good afternoon). It felt a bit like being royalty, sometimes.

The villagers would approach me using their hands actively in a vigorous beckoning gesture, as if to say, 'Come here, come here.' Then the *luluai* and perhaps some of the other more able men would throw their arms around my waist in a bear hug and lift me right off the ground. This was pretty startling and even frightening until I got used to it. These men would then repeatedly call out words that to me sounded like 'Ee *chan a vay, ee chan a vay.*'

Despite being a land so rich in languages (some 800 different ones at one count), with my having a great interest in non-English languages and perhaps because *tok pisin* was so universal, I actually picked up very little of the Highlands languages. This phrase, because it was used so expressively and so widely by the villagers, is about the only one I remember now. I did some 'research' to find out what it meant. This revealed that the word-for-word translation is 'I eat your excreta.' This, of course, is not what the villagers literally meant. It seems to have been a way of expressing the depth of their regard and affection for someone. It would be used in the same way that the pidgin word '*bel*' (belly) symbolises the seat of the emotions. An angry person would be *belhot* (hot bellied).

I imagine that the greeting given to me so enthusiastically has lost its original meaning of consumption of faeces. One might see it as akin to the way 'bloody' is claimed to arise from the somewhat blasphemous expression 'by our lady' or as in 'Goodbye!' derived from 'God be with you.'

Not that it was always sweetness and light. I certainly had my low moments. Take this whinge for instance:

Sunday 2nd December 1956: I have been very disappointed here at Yufiyufa by the dishonourable attitude of the village officials concerning pine planting. On Tuesday, we had a full discussion on the matter, and all agreed that they would be able to plant the trees starting on Thursday. They were all very emphatic that I should not distribute the seedlings to other groups or Europeans as they would all be planted out by the Yufiyufa.

However, hardly a soul turned up on Thursday, and as I write – this Sunday morning, December 2nd – I would say that of four and a half thousand pine seedling, only about two hundred have been planted. I would not have been let down in my faith in these people if they had stated outright on Tuesday that they did not wish to plant. But to promise faithfully and then completely dishonour that promise – well, it threw me into one of those moods I get sometimes.

Why try to help these people? Why don't I go back to Australia to farming where effort is rewarded even if not financially, then by the thought that you are doing something that is useful and productive.

Of course, this fit of pique occurred well before I became aware that these 'lazy' people had been cultivating that very soil, without degrading it unduly, for some 40,000 or more years! And, in due course, I recovered my patience and my enthusiasm for whatever my mission might be.

Decision-making

Politics and governance in the Papua New Guinea Highlands were very democratic compared with the structure and practice of other Pacific Islander societies. Jared Diamond puts it well:

...New Guinea highland societies represent an ultra-democratic extreme of bottom-up decision-making. Until the arrival of Dutch and Australian colonial government in the 1930s, there had not been even any beginnings of political unification in any part of the highlands: merely individual villages alternating between fighting each other and joining in temporary alliances with each other against other nearby villages. Within each village instead of hereditary leaders or chiefs, there were just individuals, called 'big men' who by force of personality were more influential than other individuals but still lived in a hut like everybody else's and tilled a garden like anybody else's. Decisions were (and often still are today) reached by everybody in the village sitting down together and talking and talking and talking. The big men couldn't give orders and they might or might not succeed in persuading others to adopt their proposals. To outsiders today (including not just me but often New Guinea government officers themselves), that bottom-up approach to decision-making can be frustrating because you can't go to some designated village leader; you have to have the patience to endure talk-talk-talk for hours or days with every villager who has some opinion to offer.

I was frequently, as one of those 'government officers', caught up in these situations as I sought to promote different farming solutions. I recorded one example, although not related specifically to agriculture:

Saturday, 15 December 1956: ...over the weekend, two men – Pepe, the government interpreter and Soso, a local luluai – passed through Notafona and gave an address on what they had seen and heard on their visit to Lae to see the Duke of Edinburgh. They brought with them news that the Duke had told them to concentrate on three things:

1. On serving the law of the Government
2. Obeying the law of God and building and use of schools
3. Regular work and the establishment of businesses.

The Villagers

I have never seen native people listen to a talk as much as these people did to Pepe and Soso. It went on for nearly five hours.

Village Talk Show
Everyone has a say.

One thing that strikes me as curious about this interlude is the store that the villagers placed on the presence and words of British royalty. It is hard to think of any institution that could be further from the conceptions and experiences of a highlands villager than a European monarchy. This acceptance of the constitutional monarchy continues to this day. Although Papua New Guinea now has its own awards system for public recognition in most fields, there remains provision for the Queen to set a quota of imperial honours for bestowal on Papua New Guinean citizens, a tradition that Australia abandoned years ago.

Given that chieftainship is not a feature of most Papua New Guinea language groups, this is rather puzzling. I suspect that having a person highly regarded in common by all citizens and beyond the tensions of adversarial politics (Papua New Guinea has also adopted the Westminster system of government), the recognition of the Queen (now, King) contributes to a sense of unity to the whole country.

As something of a counter to this, for good or ill, this democratic model was bypassed by the colonial authorities. This was most likely for administrative convenience. Following the practice, in the pre-war German colony, the Australian administration introduced the appointment of village leaders, known respectively as *luluais or tul tuls*. Loosely, the luluai was the nominal leader of the village and the tul tul his deputy. Comparisons might be President and Secretary, or King and Prime Minister. You will notice in the photograph of the group at the medical clinic the badges on the forehead and chest of the *luluai* and *tul tul*.

Greetings from Village Leaders.

Dr William Mira, an associate and past president of the Australian Numismatic Society, had described the Tultul and Luluai badges as a unique part of PNG history during the German and later the Australian administrative era:

> *These badges are and will be the only tangible reminder of Papua New Guinea's period of colonial administration.*

The system of government created the Tultul and Luluai institution during the German administration, 'This was later continued by the Australian administration until the Pacific War,' said Dr Mira.

The institution of Tultul and Luluai did not present their members with badges until after the highlands of New Guinea were explored...

Electoral registration – Lae 1964

This picture was taken some 9 years after the events related in this book. It illustrates the hats used as badges of office by *luluais* from the Papua New Guinea coast rather than the metal badges signifying the same rank in the highlands. It also demonstrates the rapid conversion to cheaper and more convenient cotton fabrics for everyday dress as shown by the woman in the picture which I imagine will be now be pretty well universal in the highlands provinces as well.

…It became obvious that the wigs and ornate hair style worn by many warriors precluded the use of caps,[displayed in most early photos of coastal village leaders]. The badges were introduced because of this.

The unique badges that were issued during the Australian administration also had two (2) 2mm holes, 'one was drilled at 9 o'clock and the other at 3 o'clock,' marking the sides of the badges, as described by Dr Mira.

These holes could be worn around the wigs of the warriors, later did a third hole appear at the top of the badges, 'later the size of the hole increased to 3mm, a third hole was then drilled at the top part of the badges, at 12 o'clock.'

Before the independence of Papua New Guinea in 1975, more and more badges were worn around the neck and the 'cap-phase' (wearing it around the head), became phased out before the independence, which also saw the introduction of Local Government Council badges.

The Luluais and Tultuls cherished their badges, and it is a reminder of Papua New Guinea's colonial era.

Aid Posts

From the illustration, the fellow with the red singlet would have been the aid post orderly for the village aid post, which you can see in the background. Such medical facilities were a measure of the welfare facilities introduced to the villages by the Australian administration. As with the patrol officers, trained medical assistants would circulate from village to village every now and then to support the aid post orderlies and bring medical supplies to do what they could with limited resources to bring a healthier life to these stone-age people.

Everyday Dress

The reader will notice in a good proportion of the pictures and text of this work a lot of reference is made to the attire of the highlands villagers up to the late 1950s. This is because what the people wore up to that time was truly distinctive. Still, a few years later, my brother Kerry in his memoir could note from a visit to the Papua New Guinea Highlands:[7]

…the villagers did not wear European clothing, men using leaves front and back, and women were bare-breasted with some form of grass skirt from the waist…the amazing thing was to see the everyday wearing of decorations particularly by the males. Although it is well-known that they paint their bodies for sing sings *and special occasions, this was surprising.*

I have not been back to the Highlands since those two short years, but I gather from recent photographs – for instance of the Missionary Aviation Fellowship landing aeroplanes in remote areas – that the old decorative dress has been fully replaced by the cheaper and perhaps more durable clothes of the trade stores and supermarkets. And I notice that it is rare for Papua New Guinea women now to go bare-breasted, except occasionally in dance performances. Curiously, though, this applies even to coastal areas such as the famed Trobriand Islands. I came across a picture recently of a dancing group from the so-called Islands of Love showing the young woman participants all clothed with cotton bras.

---

[7] Kerry Eivers, My Magic Carpet Ride, p. 82.

Dressing Up

Waist band and cloak of *tapa* cloth, head bands of seeds or small shells, arm bands sheathing pig or cassowary bones and pendant of mother-of-pearl shell.

Young Man in Everyday Attire.

This rather serious-looking young bloke provides a further example of the customary apparel for highlanders at that time. The head piece would be of parrot feathers, seeds or possibly small shells, edged with possum or tree kangaroo (*kapul*) fur. The beads of the sash would be of a hollow cane grass and the neckpiece of pearl shell traded in from the coast over time. The use of pearl shell as currency and for decoration comes originally from the coastal Papua New Guinea tribes, especially from the Kuanua language group near Rabaul. Somehow, despite the isolation of the mountain tribes, the *kina* was traded inland before the European's opening up of the interior. It is, however, possible that this youth's neck piece came from shell distributed to the local peoples by European traders as a means of payment for various goods and services. For the highlanders, the shell would have been a more valuable currency in those early days of contact than what was available as legal tender.

Noticeable are the clearly visible arm bands on the wrists. These most likely, at this stage of law enforcement, would have been purely decorative. One could speculate, however, that they also played a military role as an arm guard in the use of the bow and arrow. In 1955, there was still a fair bit of inter-tribal fighting going on, and in the event of these, the traditional bows and arrows were brought into use. The bow was made of a black palm timber and with a string of cane.

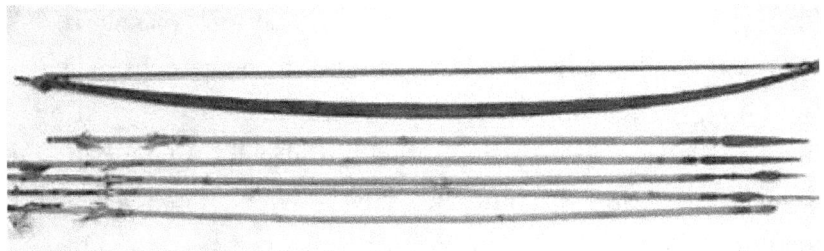

Photo Internet

These weapons had nowhere near the power of the Mediaeval English long bow or those of the Mongols and other war-prone people. They could still cause fatal damage, however. This may have been as much from the bacterial infection they facilitated as for the physical deadly piercing of body organs.

The most common use of these weapons, though, probably still likely today, would have been for the hunting of game for food and (especially birds of paradise) for plumes. An even more common employment even in 1955 would have been for display, ceremony and dancing.

As well as the weapons of attack, there were defensive devices employed by the villagers.

Tuesday, 19 February 1957:

Ian came round to my shelter and showed me one of the spikes these people plant in their gardens to discourage barefooted trespassers. An instance where a policeman was speared in the foot with one of these was shown in the film 'Walk into Paradise.' I have come across these spikes up at Miruma, but this is the first time I have seen them in this end of the valley. They are certainly nasty things, being made out of bamboo splinters and vary from four to twelve inches long.

Although not clear from the photograph, this young man may be wearing around his nether regions a 'skirt' of braided string made, as with those of the girls and women, from one of the common fibres such as paper mulberry tree (also beaten into *tapa* cloth). At other times especially for day to day use in the gardens or when travelling, as seen in other pictures, he is likely to be wearing a branch of *tanget* (*Cordilyne* spp.) held in place by a fibre belt and discreetly covering the buttocks. It was a very much renewable item of clothing for their wardrobe, because the *tanget* also played a role as a fencing material. A fresh bunch was readily available to be plucked at will from the gardens and from the 'fencing' at the side of the walking tracks.

Tanget was a commonly used fibre and sheeting material. This plant, botanically mainly *Cordyline fruticosa*, is common throughout the Indo-pacific, and has had many utilitarian and ceremonial functions.

C. fruticosa (*tanget* in *tok pisin*) is closely allied to the Australian species of *Cordyline* and is the northernmost of a north-south series of species from Cape York (Queensland) to New South Wales. It is native to lands neighbouring Cape York along the Bismarck Archipelago (where there is a wide range of natural variation) and perhaps to islands further north (Micronesia) and continental areas further west as far as Burma. It may also be native to Cape York itself. However, the exact indigenous distribution has been complicated by human dispersal and selection. The species has been carried throughout Polynesia and Melanesia as far as Hawaii, Easter Island and New Zealand and has been selected into innumerable cultivars reflecting a wide range of uses in food, medicine, textiles and religion.

Various *Cordyline species* are common garden plants in Queensland, and here is a sample taken from my own garden.

You will notice the long stem supporting the bunch of leaves. These stems provided the 'palings' for the fences keeping the pigs out of the gardens. The leaves were left growing out of the top to provide a living fence or hedge. If a young man wanted to freshen up his appearance, he would simply snap

Tanget
Photo R Eivers 2021

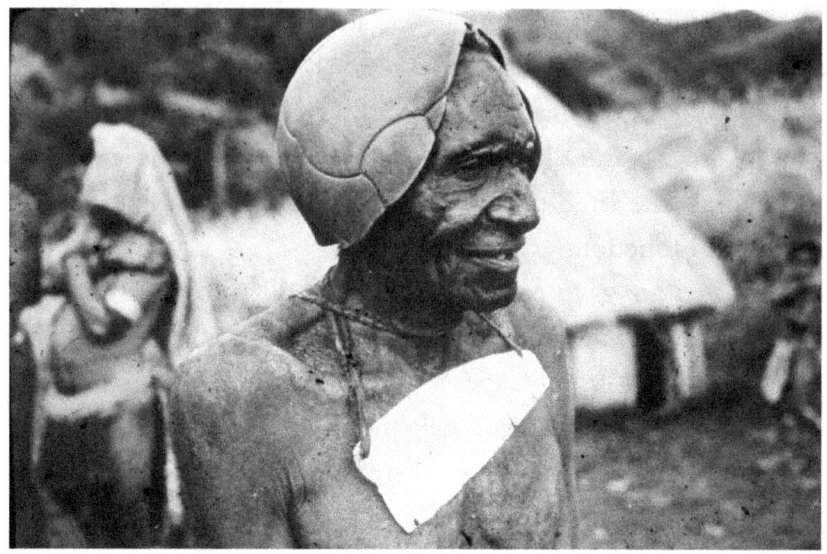

PhotoR Eivers 2021
A Modern Adaptation (regrettable in my opinion) of Traditional Garb

off a bunch of leaves of the *tanget*, as we were walking past the garden and tuck them behind him under his belt.

For those of us in fields as wide as anthropology and colonial administration who have found something valuable and beautiful in traditional arts and crafts of indigenous people, we face the conundrum of how we do not lose – or perhaps suppress – their initiatives, their cultural facility, especially in the arts and clothing, while introducing the people to the clear benefits of western technology. Part of the hope of this book has been to show the common usage of home-made traditional dress still prevalent in the highlands as late as the 1950s.

Nowadays, as far as I know, the traditional adornment has been swamped by mass-produced fabrics from the cheap-labour mills, especially of the developing Asian countries.

On one level, though, as I have noticed from pictures of other preliterate cultures, the availability of cheap colourful materials such as body paint has led to ceremonial and entertainment attire being more spectacular than ever. I suspect, though even more regrettably, that with the availability of shot guns replacing the bow and arrow, far more birds are being shot and killed to provide the feathers adorning the dancers in the public *sing sings*. These dancing and chanting performances now probably cater to tourism to a significant degree. From the television news reports one views from time to time it does seem that the 'commercialisation' of tourism has led to celebratory display of dress and dancing growing to have no less a prominent place in the new national culture.

The next group of pictures shows villagers all dressed up for such a *sing sing*. It is to be noted that the remarkable thing about these photographs is that they were taken in the village setting and not for a display for tourists. Presumably the rationale for the dressing up was for local ceremonial purposes and perhaps, as with the pork feasts, some measure of conspicuous consumption.

Checking the Drum Kit

The Villagers

A Friendlier Artefact – Jews Harp

This musical instrument produces a twanging or humming sound. It comprises a length of bamboo, slit down one side, with a very thin tongue of bamboo up the middle of the slit. This sliver is plucked or blown over the open mouth to resonate and generate the musical notes.

While the pictures preceding this one, and others depicted elsewhere, displayed the bows and arrows used in hunting or warfare, there were a number of other tools and instruments development for entertainment and ceremony by the villagers. The hour-glass-shaped drum (*kundu*) always accompanied the chanting and dancing. The slit log drum (*garamut*) could be found, although not as common as in several other provinces of the country.

Who Needs a Barber Shop?
Hairdressing utensils included combs of bamboo, and tweezers – also of bamboo – were used to pluck out unruly hairs.

Children's Entertainment

A Good Chew – Sugar Cane Interlude

Village Life

Papua New Guinea Domesticity – The Woman of the House
The Village Kitchen (mumu)

We have here an example of the steam cooking of food through heated stones. Other Pacific Islanders use the same principle as did highlanders, but they dig a pit in the ground to form the oven in which to place the uncooked food and the heated rocks.

In this case, the lady has her own hollowed-out log as an oven. She is sensibly using a pair of bamboo tongs to handle the stones, and on the left, you can see the length of hollowed-out bamboo for carrying water to generate the steam.

The food prepared and lying on the ground would be maize (an introduced crop but already grown very widely), edible *pit pit* and sweet potato (*kau kau)*.

Sweet potato - kau kau
Photo: Internet

The regular diet did not have much animal protein in it. Every village, probably every household, had its own pigs, virtually kept as pets (see elsewhere) until time for slaughter.

Faintly, you can just see a village pig between the two Casuarina trees on the far right of the picture. The killing of pigs for food took place mainly for ceremony and ostentatious displays at the periodical feasts. For such feasts, the pig owners would bring in their animals trussed up and swung from a pole on the shoulders of a man at the front and one at the back. The animals would then be lined up in a row through the middle of the village. The pigs were killed by a blow of a log of wood to the snout.

To a young sensitive Australian such as me whose knowledge of butchering (despite the valuable farm experience from Muresk Agricultural College) was what you bought in 'dressed' form from the local butcher shop, this practice seemed a bit brutal and somewhat repugnant. Nevertheless, it was probably no more painful to the creatures than the captive bolt pistol used in commercial abattoirs.

To a first observer such as me, this seemed a bit crude and cruel, particularly when the animals were not stunned at the first blow. And, of course, the villagers did not have access to guns or other more sophisticated means of turning live creatures into food for humans.

Although I did not see much of this, there would also be game from hunting – birds and tree kangaroos, for instance.

There would be the occasional rat thrown into the home fires commonly found burning on the floor inside the houses or in the village grounds. I was invited to try a sample of rat and did rather tentatively have a taste. It was nothing unexpected, perhaps, and being well cooked in the fire by then, the leg or whatever it was I consumed had a rather pleasant roasted flavour.

The fires were inside the houses to provide warmth in that sub-alpine climate. You can see from the background of the picture how compact the houses were. They were not always of that size. On occasion, when it was raining, I shared some time in these houses with the villagers. They were cosy, but the comfort depended on how much smoke was being generated by the fire that was kept going in the middle of the house. I suspect that this ever-present smokiness had deleterious effects on the long-term health of the occupiers.

> *Friday, March 1st, 1957:*
>
> *We are at present at the Hagaulo rest house, which according to the altimeter is 7,000 feet above sea level. Judging by the night temperature, one can well believe it.*
>
> *I was quite comfortable in a newly built 'round house,' but I think Harry and Ian suffered as their beds were in the square house, a type which although quite useful in lowland areas is certainly not a suitable design for these higher altitudes.*

No matches to get a fire going? No problem!

The villagers were keen to show me how they readily make fire. Variations of this process go way back through time and were presumably practiced by our European ancestors. In rubbing a hard wood against a soft wood in the presence of readily flammable tinder, Native Americans used the bow drill that gave them the extra leverage in twirling a hard stick on the softwood surface. Australian Aborigines achieved the same response by twirling the stick by hand. I expect that the vigorous action required in this instance provided for the development of blisters and eventually some protective calluses of the skin.

The highlanders used a different approach. They would excavate a little hole in the earth for the tinder and cover this with the small length of softwood. They would then take a strip of cane from the forest, perhaps of lawyer vine about 50 cm long, and pass it under the slab of softwood. Then with a hand on each end, the cane was drawn quickly up and down from side to side. The friction from this created sparks. These would fall down on to the tinder, and with some puffing of breath as encouragement, the tinder would catch alight and away we would go.

Pre-European Foods

Sweet Potato

Sweet Potato *(kau kau)* is very much the staple source of starch-based carbohydrate in the Highlander diet. It plays the comparative role of rice in Asia and potatoes in Ireland

Marita

The food being prepared here is the fruit of a Pandanus plant *(Pandanus conoideus),* which seems to be endemic to the island of New Guinea and nowhere else. This fruit forms along the flower spike, much as with maize. The fleshy surround is removed from the stem, as seen in the picture, and then heated and formed into a liquid with very much the appearance of tomato sauce. It does not have the salty flavour of our sauces or soups, and care has to be taken that it is not consumed too much, because it can generate insomnia. At maturity, its deep red colour reveals a high level of beta-carotene and is thus a precursor of Vitamin A with consequent benefits to health. The lack of salty flavour may well have been accepted by choice, but more likely, the taste for it had developed over the centuries when, with the locations being so far from the coast, salt was a rare commodity.

Fencing – Mainly to Keep the Pigs Out
Utilising *pit pit,* a cane grass something like a small bamboo.

Pork

Live pigs, although ever-present in the villages, as noted above, and indeed in the homes, were not routinely slaughtered for food. As can be seen in a number of pictures in this volume, they filled a role – one might say – as family pets. They were well looked after, even though their owners were fully aware that they would end up as food when fully grown. Their most critical role was not so much as a source of nutrients but for display and measure of wealth. To display and exchange the animals or the pork derived from them created a measure of affluence and probably networks of obligation.

Introduced Foods

Mixed Vegetables – Sweet Potato in the Foreground

Sweet potato, originating from South America, seems in a roundabout way to have been introduced to the Papua New Guinea 1200 years ago. So well established has it become, though, that it now supplies as much as 65 percent of the carbohydrate component of rural diets. Other food crops have been introduced much later than that but have established themselves well in the farming pattern. Sugar cane has been mentioned elsewhere. Bananas also are well established with a wide range of varieties.

Maize – Indian Corn

A crop arriving circuitously in the Pacific via Europe from its origin in Mexico, maize has the highest production of cereal grain throughout the world, greater even than wheat or rice.

Maize and paw paw, as with bananas, were largely unfamiliar to me as a common food, being raised in Western Australia with its cooler more temperate climate and a Western European culture that did not incorporate them in the daily diet.

My first memory of tasting 'corn on the cob' comes from sitting around the village campfire in the Highlands while on patrol and having the folk around me throw a few corn cobs into the ashes. When offered to me to eat, I experienced a pleasant, toasted flavour that since then has led to my continuing to enjoy corn cob consumption, now in subtropical Queensland.

Irish potatoes may well have been introduced by the European incursion, but fresh quantities of this were readily available by 1955. Given abundant supplies of the familiar sweet potato, the local people may not have taken to the taste of the Irish potato crop but used it mainly as a source of income from the resident Europeans. To meet the growing demand from people in the towns and cities, most of the potatoes consumed in Papua New Guinea these days would be imports, mainly from Australia.

Banana

Bananas were perhaps the most obvious fruit plant in the number and variety in Papua New Guinea gardens. Beyond the many cultivars found in the horticultural cycle, there are many wild varieties to be found in the forest across the country. There were certainly hundreds of different types and archaeological records especially from Kup excavations in the neighbouring Western Highlands Province indicate that they have been cultivated for some 7,000 to 10,000 years. This would then mark them has having been grown for food for longer here than anywhere else in the world

Bananas Transplanting

Bananas off to Market or for Exchange

Female Fashion

Young Girl Child's String Dress and Kina Shell – Asaro River

The Villagers

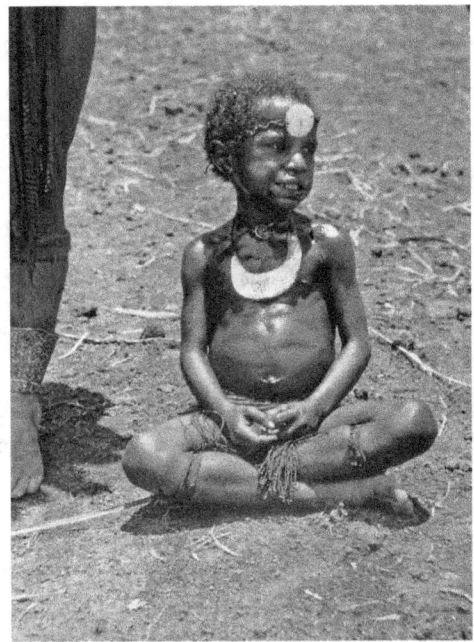

All Oiled Up

This child with her customary traditional dress has supplemented her adornment with a coating of oil. The oil is probably of plant origin, perhaps *marita (Pandanus conoideus)*. While *marita* has some value as a food, it may also be that the oiling of the skin provides some warmth for the people at these regions and the altitudes at which this Pandanus seems to be solely found.

String Bag – *Bilum*

Travelling in Comfort and Style

When it was time for a rest the *bilum*, with the baby, would be hung on the branch of a convenient tree, allowing the child to swing gently in the breeze.

Mothering with Fashion
'Skirt' of tapa cloth (beaten Mulberry bark) and woven bilum.
Rock-a-bye baby.

Proud Father

Or at least a wealthy, one judging by the layers of pearl shell with which he has adorned his daughter

A Woman's Work is Never Done! – Multitasking, Highlander Style

Pets

The main domesticated animals kept in the villages were scrawny-looking dogs and especially pigs. These sometimes had a run of the village but had to be kept out of the food gardens that were routinely fenced with Casuarina (She-oak) or *tanget* stakes.

Piglet Members of the Family

The pigs were valuable items and were treated with care amounting to their being regarded as family pets until they met their ends in the conspicuous consumption of ceremonial slaughter. So valuable were they and so highly regarded that the piglets were encouraged to suckle at the breasts of their human mistresses.

The villagers, moreover, especially in the richly forested areas, lived in an environment harbouring accessible wildlife. Tree kangaroos and birds of paradise were prime examples. While the adult animals would be a source of food or body decoration, the young animals were often kept for a while essentially as pets. Some examples are provided in the pictures here.

The Villagers

Bird with Cage

Cassowary Chick
Photo: R Eivers 1963

CHAPTER NINE
Interracial Coupling

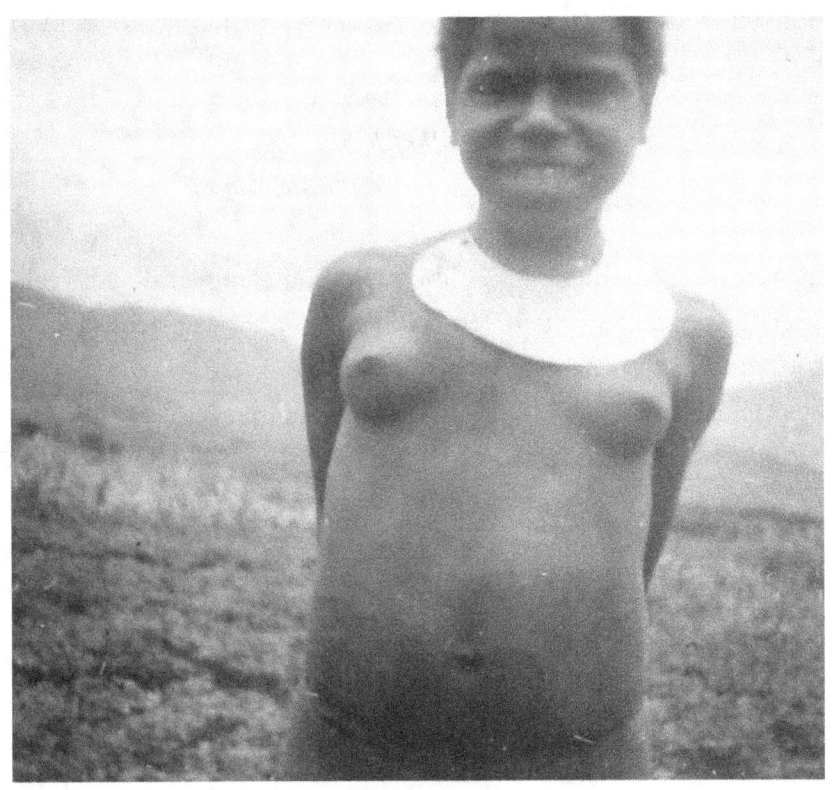

GONEGIRI
(Gohnaygeeri)

The poor quality of this photo can be attributed to my struggles with a camera that I had bought by post only a few weeks prior to this. In these days of digital photography, one can ascertain immediately the quality of one's efforts. At that time, I developed and printed my own photographs and may have failed to get some of the processing timings right. Later with the colour films, however, one had to wait until the roll of film was finished, then send it away to be developed and printed, and then when the slides arrived in the post, only then could one tell whether or not one had made a mess of it!

The back of the original photograph has the intriguing inscription:

March 1956
GONEGIRI of KOFENA
Offered to me as a bride.

In preparing for this book and discovering this picture 65 years after it was taken, I was left wondering what lay behind it. I consulted my journal from that time:

Monday, 12 March 1956:
Last Thursday, one of the local Kofena tul tuls must have thought I looked lonely, for he offered me his sister to be my wife. I declined the offer, with thanks of course, as I never know when I am likely to settle down, and it certainly won't be for a while yet. I also explained that I had several female friends back in Australia [though I should say, nowhere at the stage of serious courtship].

I thought it would interest the folks back home, so today, I went down and took two snapshots of the girl, Gonegiri by name. As local people go, she is quite good-looking and very well formed. I can't honestly say I wasn't interested, for it is true, one becomes very starved of female company up here, and as Toby Boito remarked one day, figu-

Interracial Coupling

ratively speaking of course, 'The skins of the native girls get paler every day you are with them.'

If I don't marry a native girl, it certainly won't be because of the colour of her skin. I would not hesitate if I happened to become very attached to one who was intelligent and very well educated. I am far from ready to settle down and marry just yet.

There are many settlers in the Highlands who do have native wives, though in most cases, they are kept for sexual satisfaction rather than companionship. Joe Searson (former patrol officer) and Jim Taylor (former district commissioner) are among those with native wives in the Goroka District.

Clearly, the idea of my marrying young Gonegiri was ridiculous, given the vast cultural difference between the two of us. I would, at that stage, have not known a word of her language, for a start. At the age of 20 years, going straight from a male-only college in the West Australian countryside, with very little contact with young Australian women and an attitude that marriage was an ultimate aim and that sexual intimacy was to be reserved for marriage, I was in no position to tie myself to a young stone-age girl.

But let us look at the purpose of the villagers and presumably her family who made this offer. There may be some significance in that I actually was given, and recorded, her name. The naming of those in photographs did not happen in any of the other pictures I took of village people at that time.

The villagers, however, may have taken this offer seriously.

What was in it for them? I had nothing to offer. Even though a government officer, I had virtually no legal power as possessed, say, by the *kiaps*. By using the term 'bride,' was the intention more of merely a sexual coupling – a one night stand?

In reflecting on this with a friend, also with former experience in the highlands of Papua New Guinea, he wondered if the potential for a substantial 'bride price' was behind Wasime's enthusiasm for the matrimonials. Certainly, the system of bride pricing is common in Papua New Guinea, including the highlands. It is said to occur with some two-thirds of households, and recently, the rate has reached $20,000–$30,000 or more. Nevertheless, such monetary considerations for Gonegiri's hand were not raised or hinted at in my conversations with Wasime.

In all my time in Papua New Guinea, I had never been sexually solicited by a woman. I was never aware of any casual sexual coupling by other Papua New Guinea government officers, although we can be pretty confident that it occurred from time to time, especially in the more 'sophisticated' coastal regions of the country. At the same time, the villagers may have been aware that several Australians from the early explorers in the 1930s had settled around Goroka and Mount Hagen and established a variety of agricultural and pastoral enterprises, including coffee and beef. Among these would have been the Leahy, Fox and Taylor families.

Although some tension developed in later years over alienation of villagers' land to the white settlers, this was not evident at the time I was there. It is possible that the villagers willingly transferred land to wealthy outsiders as a matter of prestige or perhaps of stimulating the provision of infrastructure and commercial services.

It has frequently occurred with the European invasion of colonial lands that misunderstanding over land purchases has arisen because Europeans see such transactions as leading to outright ownership and control of a parcel of land. For many indigenous people, however, a purchase represented the right to use the land and often for only a given period of time.

In relation to our topic of sexual coupling, these settlers did indeed marry local village women. These liaisons, whether de facto or registered, led to 'dynasties' that continue to play a large part in Papua New Guinea commercial and civic life.

With Gonegiri, I politely declined the offer, and we shall never know what prompted the gesture from the people of Kofena. It would be nice to think that it was an extension of the warmth with which they welcomed me by other means into their communities.

Some days after I had written the above response to the photograph of Gonegiri, I happened to glance again through one of my journals at the time and discovered that there was a little more to her story than that. It seems that Gonegiri's brother did not let up. This was my note for 24 April 1956, some seven weeks after the previous entry:

> *In the evening, I had a visit from a character, Wasime by name of Kofena. Apparently, he wants me to marry this girl Gonegiri, for he says, 'Her love for me is strong,' or words to that effect. More down to earth was his proposal to lend me some ground to grow peanuts for sale. The only thing I would have to do would be to pay for some labourers. At the same time, they would help Wasime to work the ground and a build a fence for his coffee garden. It sounds interesting, and I'll look the place over and make a decision when I go up to Kofena. I'm not sure what the position is with working a small business on the side when in the public service.*

Well, I don't know what the outcome of this proposed little venture was. I have no more record of what happened to Gonegiri. From an experience some 20 years later when I enquired about real property ownership while in the public service, I am pretty sure the 'business on the side' would have received an emphatic 'No!' from my employers.

One observation of interest from this little episode is that it confirms that the local people at that time were not averse to making land available or going into business with the invasive white folk. Indeed, they may have seen these partnerships as being a source of potential wealth. Later on, there did arise some tension from misunderstandings over land alienation.

That was pretty well the end of the story except, for a couple of notes later recorded:

29 April 1956: I gave Gonegiri her photo, but she is still pretty shy.

5 May 1956: …planting out coffee again, mainly replacement at Kofena. Gonegiri was there helping with the work. '

Sorcery and Violence

Although I have repeated that I felt no threat of aggression, armed or otherwise, during my perambulating of the highlands villages, I may not have felt the same confidence if I had repeated the visitations in later years. There were no guns in the hands of the local people up to the 1950s, but not long after that, some men were provided with licences for shot guns. Inter-tribal tensions continued to break out in local warfare, and in due course, the villagers used some initiative to construct their own guns. There are now gun ownership regulations legislated in the country, but this does not seem to be the sensitive issue it has been in Australia since the Port Arthur massacre by Martin Bryant. In view of the difficulties of secure storage of firearms, it is perhaps surprising that they do not feature more in inter-tribal stoushes.

Regarding sorcery and witchcraft, it is easy to forget how much the threat of supernatural interaction with a dangerous spiritual world plays on the mind of people in most cultures. With our Western scientific analysis and testing of hypotheses and the benefits of secular education, the belief in evil from unknown presences outside our control hangs over us less and less. Not that it is altogether absent in our own society when one considers the attention given to horoscopes and other paranormal phenomena beyond the scope of scientific understanding by readers of our newspapers and other sources.

For people like those of our villagers who have had no access to these modern 'rational' interpretations of the events in their lives – particularly when it comes to illness, for example – the fear of harmful spiritual influences can be very real indeed.

In my patrolling of the outlying locations, there were a number of occasions on which my staff would not enter certain villages or localities because of strong uneasiness about a reputed source of sorcery – *poison* in pidgin.

CHAPTER TEN
Patrol Facilities

In looking back over 65 years and recalling the highlights of one's experience, I find myself vainly trying to pinpoint some of the more mundane but necessary elements of life under these circumstances. Where and when did I urinate, for instance, on those long 7–9 hours walks when out in the open air and in the company of others, both men and women. And what sort of meals did I have? I have no penchant for cooking or food preparation, and I presume the work on this was done by my house servant who accompanied me on the patrols, or by one of the agricultural assistants. Perhaps I shared meals with them sometimes. To some degree, it may have been with the villagers. Corn cobs had never been part of my diet under traditional West Australian cuisine, but on the highlands patrols, I was introduced to this taste that I continue to enjoy today. It was very easy when sitting around a fire in the middle of the village to have a few cobs tossed into the ashes and develop their roasted flavour. I have mentioned elsewhere my sampling the roasted leg of a rat.

Too Many Apples a Day

In preparing for time away from the town, I would have had to order the provisions myself. The main meat source was wedge-shaped tins of corned beef. One of my choices on one occasion had very uncomfortable consequences. I developed a taste for dried apple, which besides being tasty did not require preservatives or take up much room in the limited space of our patrol boxes. I got to chewing on this dried apple rather than adding water and cooking it. One evening, perhaps while getting caught up in some compelling reading, I got stuck into my bag of dried apple.

After retiring to bed, around about midnight, I started to feel very uncomfortable in my middle region. Although there was not much pain, a rumbling began and continued to get worse. Realising that something had to give, I staggered out the open door of the *haus kiap* into the village compound and then threw up and discharged large lumps of undigested apple over the ground outside.

I had had no expectation of such a result, and at the time, it got me thinking. In my childhood, I had read a story – one of those with a very moralistic thrust told to children of the 19th and early 20th centuries. The tale goes something like this. A mischievous boy reaches over a fence and steals a farmer's apples. He eats one or more apples and later finds himself with a severe belly ache. The moral of this story, of course, is, 'It serves him right.'

So, up to this point – brought up as I was in the apple-growing heartland in South-Western Australia – any link between apples and illness was never hinted at. It was more a case of 'an apple a day keeps the doctor away.' This experience indicated to me that there is something in apples that is purgative. I quickly learned to ease back on my consumption of this fruit, remaining to this day an 'apple a day' man.

Accommodation

Village 'Guest House' (Haus Kiap)
Photo: Kerry Eivers 1964

A building such as this, lined up with or surrounded integrally with the villagers' traditional round houses, was a standard feature in villages as a requirement by the Australian administration. It was used to accommodate visiting government officers. With appropriate acceptance by the villagers, it could also be available to other visitors such as missionaries and, I suspect, perhaps increasingly today, by tourists. As might be expected, with such accommodation, one had to bring one's own lighting and plumbing facilities. The hurricane and Tilley lamps have already been described. Bathing was provided from a shower bucket, of canvas in my case, hung from the ceiling.

The grass thatch for roof and plaited cane grass for walls can be clearly seen in the picture. The floor – in contrast to the village houses – was built off the ground. The floor was also of 'bamboo.' And thereby hangs my tale.

Haus Kiap Under Construction

Haus Kiap – The Finished Product

Midnight Drama

Despite being in the tropics, it can be very cold at night. Remember, some of these Highlands villages were situated at altitudes as high as 2500 metres – 300 metres higher than Mt Kosciusko, at about 2200 metres up. To keep the guests warm in the houses and to provide a fire for cooking, a layer of clay was built above the cane floor. This 'fireplace' was about a metre square and was edged with small rocks on which one could support a billy can or other cooking utensils. The fire was built on the stratum of clay sitting on the cane floor.

One night, I retired to bed as usual, checking that the fire was safe and just smouldering and glowing enough to keep some warmth outside the blankets.

Around midnight, I woke up sensing that something was not quite right. To my horror, I noticed that flames were licking and advancing along the floor matting. I jumped out of bed, raced outside and probably shouted out for my assisting staff and the villagers who would have been sleeping nearby. I use the phrase 'probably shouted,' because I am sometimes to my own surprise, not a shouting person. Whatever way it happened, however, I managed to get people's attention, and they came running to my aid.

My main recollection is of going back into the house – the flames had been beaten out at this stage – and urinating on the embers in a presumably desperate attempt to extinguish the potential for any more flames. I doubt that this made much impression on the abundance of hot coals. Clearly, though, the people from the neighbouring quarters had managed to beat out the remaining flames with wet branches and whatever else came to hand. There would have been no other fire prevention facilities in that village situation.

What had happened, of course, was that the bed of the fireplace had been so hot that the temperature had become high enough to set the underlying floor matting alight. The flames had then edged along horizontally till, with greater feed of cane matting fuel from the walls they had become sufficient to set the main building alight. It may well be that this sort of incident happened more often than enough and, perhaps with other individuals, with tragic results.

I described it thus at the time:

Tuesday, 8 May 1956: Tonight, I came as close to death as I have ever have before, probably. I had gone to bed after working with my newly arrived stamps when the lamp ran out of kerosene. I was asleep at about half past three. I heard a crackling and woke up thinking that the fire shouldn't be doing that when I had only left big logs on it. I really woke up then and raced round to the front room to see one wall of the house in flames. I was happy to note that my first honest thoughts were that I should give thanks to God for waking. Possibly another five seconds would have been too late, for the flames were just starting on the highly inflammable grass roof when I grabbed up a towel and managed to beat them off. I was in the back room, and this is one of the few rest houses with solid plank walls. I wouldn't have had a hope if the fire had sealed off the front room. It'll certainly teach me to be more careful with fires in the future.

Village Residence Under Construction
Note the compact circular shape for maximum warmth

Photo: Postcard
A Happy Pose! At Home Sweet Home
The house walls of cane and roof of grass thatch can be clearly seen.

Children's Companionship

Young children seemed to have a relaxed and happy time. There was no formal education, and not much seemed to be demanded of them until they reached their teens. Even so, very young children could be seen helping their adult family members willingly enough with the many chores of village living and gardening. One big contrast with our Western patterns of child-raising was that there was no specific early bedtime for these children. They were allowed to play around for as late in the evening as they wished. Then, when they were tired enough, they would settle down and go to sleep. My role did not require my having any specific responsibilities with the children, but they seemed to enjoy my company. Nowadays, as was beginning to happen in the 1950s and earlier, of course, the children would be at school during the day. By now, these children that I encountered 65 years ago, would be aged and 'retired' from their western-style employment. During this single generation, they adopted and absorbed – well enough – adequate education in a foreign tongue to lift them from a stone-age culture into running a democratic government and sustainable modern economy. What an achievement!

Albino Child

One can speculate on how difficult life must have been in that environment for a child to have to cope with a skin colour so striking in contrast to that of his family and day-to-day companions. It may be reading too much into the photograph to note that he alone of all the youngsters posing here appears unhappy. It would not be correct to say that albinism is common among PNG people, but I certainly came across individuals from time to time. I have to say, as against my initial comments above, that wherever I came across albino children or adults, there was never any indication that they were other than fully accepted as natural members of their family and community.

One particular night, a group of young children up to about the age of 7 or 8 years were chatting and sitting around the fire at night inside my *haus kiap*. I just went on lying on my camp stretcher and reading a book. I was starting to think it was getting late and that it was time for me to turn in and for the children to go home to bed. I communicated this to them.

No problem! To my astonishment, the half dozen or so of the boys and girls lay down on my matting floor and cuddled beside the fire in a row, 'spooning' into one another. It was like peas in a pod or a row of piglets with their sow. That was them for the night! It became clear to me that this is one way they managed to keep warm enough to get to sleep in that cold mountain climate. Remember, they wore no clothing.

Indeed, it amazes me that the adults also wore minimum clothing and yet managed to stay alive and comfortable despite the often-frigid night air. I suppose the same mystery applies to our Australian Aborigines. In the case of the Aborigines, they did not even have the warmth of the low-set houses resided in by these highlands villagers and being relatively draft free.

Some young friends

Serenaded?

> *Monday, 14 May 1956: This evening now, as usual, I sat near a fire outside (I am not going to risk being cooked inside again) and was more or less made love to by some of the very young girls (10 to 14 years old) sitting around with the usual young boys. They have a seductive half-crying sort of playful attitude when asking you to come and sleep with them. There is not normally sexual intercourse when a boy sleeps with a girl here. It is perhaps equivalent to our customs of hugging and kissing [or even teen-aged ballroom dancing] and is allowed by the girl when she likes a boy.*

This village was at the western end of the valley adjacent to the Simbu District and the Wahgi Valley, so my observation of this courtship practice may be equivalent to what takes place in locations a little further west. A custom known as *karim lek* (carry leg) is known there. With this tradition, a girl sits on a boy's lap or alongside a boy with both her legs across one of his thighs. Both parties rub noses and usually arouse each other sexually, often to climax.

To my regret, I am not spontaneously a very playful person, and yet the children seemed to hang around me without hesitation – perhaps the curiosity of my white skin had something to do with it.

There were games they would play, but I cannot recall specific details of the actions and the rules. They did teach me how to make little 'spears' out of leaves of the *kunai* (blady grass *Imperata sp.*), which has a strong middle rib. The leaf blade is broken into a length of 15 centimetres or so. The 'wings' of the length of blade are then stripped back for about 10 cm and wound around the forefinger. The blade is then pointed at the target, perhaps an insect or tree leaf, and the finger pulled away very sharply. This action sends the midrib of the leaf blade to shoot out with some force into whatever target – if any – is selected.

CHAPTER ELEVEN

The Job

The Policy

Kim Godbold in her study outlines the overall task that was set before me with this village-to-village patrolling:

> *Prior to World War II, under Australian administration, the economic development of these two territories, as in many colonies of the time, was based on the institution of the plantation. Little was initiated in agricultural development for indigenous people. This changed after World War II to a rationale based on the promotion and advancement of primary industry but also came to include indigenous farmers.*
>
> *To develop agriculture within a colony, it was thought that a modification to, or in some cases the complete transformation of, existing farming systems was necessary to improve the material welfare of the population. It was also seen to be a guarantee for the future national interest of the sovereign state after independence was granted.*

So I, as a *didiman*, became a front line field worker for this theoretical model of development. The following are a few details of specific ventures in which I was engaged or had some association with.

Coffee

Coffee Tree

Shaded Nursery Under Construction

Shaded Coffee Nursery – Near Completion

Nearly There
Preparation of soil bedding for coffee seedlings

Coffee Seedling Nursery

Fish

An Unlikely Fish Pond!

The formal name of my employer was the Department of Agriculture, Stock and Fisheries. One can reasonably assume that there was not much place for an adviser on fisheries in the heart of the mountainous terrain of Papua New Guinea Highlands. Clearly, from the picture shown, the policymakers in Port Moresby and ourselves, as putting that policy into effect, thought it was worth a go. Despite the plentiful rain in this land, there are actually very few lakes. Kutubu, in the Southern Highlands, near the location for much oil exploration and extraction in later years, is probably the best known of any montane lakes.

A More Likely Fish Pond Site

The rationale for the fish pond venture was presumably to provide supplementary nutrients for the local diet. Although reasonably sustaining, the highlands foods lacked the degree of protein content that might have contributed to better health for the people of these hills and valleys.

Tilapia
Photo: Internet

So, within the first month or two of my assignment to the Eastern Highlands, I began an association with the construction and stocking of fish ponds. The species of fish with which the ponds were stocked was of the genus Tilapia. This species has a worldwide distribution in fish farming and is very fast growing. With such vitality, however, it has however, in many countries, Australia being a prime example, become a pest because of its competition with indigenous species. I am not sure to what extent that exercised the minds of the people who nominated this animal for our trials. Nor do I know to what extent the project achieved its purpose in this part of the country.

Water Reticulation for the Fish Pond

Channelling with plant stems such as banana and bamboo also occasionally used for village water supply

I have, however, become aware that in other environments where there is ample water, Tilapia farming has become commercialised to the extent of utilising such advanced aquaculture methods as caged fish farming. It is practised nowadays, for example, in Sirinumu Dam, the reservoir that powers the supply of electricity to the capital Port Moresby.

Finding the level – an improvised plumb bob

Anyway, back in 1955, we did our little bit. Beyond the promotion of coffee planting, the construction of shade houses as nurseries and monitoring the health of the seedlings, my on-site time seems to have been spent laying out fish ponds more than anything else. The fish were bred at Goroka and the fingerlings distributed to localised ponds around the countryside. Soon after my arrival in Goroka, my colleague Jim Sharp was assigned to visiting the neighbouring sub-district of Chuave to explore the potential for extracting bat manure from the caves there for fertilising the fish ponds.

A-frame Levelling for Fish Pond Water Reticulation

Fingerlings Released

Crop Introductions

Passion Fruit

The Australian-originated firm Cottees, established early in the 20th century, is well-known for a number of food products of a sweet nature such as carbonated drinks and dessert toppings. I remember in the 1950s when a neighbour of ours in the Western Australian suburb of Cottesloe who worked for Cottees came up to me and urged me to try their latest product. This was a chocolate-flavoured ice-cream topping. It must have caught on well. Cottees now supply some 60 percent of the sweet topping markets and indeed, with a check just now, I see we have a bottle of the chocolate variety in our pantry.

Cottees's main claim to fame, however, was a product they labelled 'Passiona.' They have been making this since 1927. The name, as it suggests, is derived from the flavour of the passion fruit, which is used as its base. The search for supplies of the fruit ingredient that has certain climatic boundaries took them to the highlands of Papua New Guinea. It may well have been hoped that the labour cost of harvesting the fruit would also favour its planting in that environment. The Department of Agriculture, Stock and Fisheries probably also saw the establishment of the industry as a step towards improving the financial livelihood of the villagers. Those familiar with passion fruit will be aware that cultivation can be very simple. Seeds are planted at the bottom of trees or of constructed trellises. A vine develops and reaches upwards. When the fruit is ripe, it simply falls to the ground and can then be picked up and eaten or processed.

With this in mind, Cottees built a processing factory at North Goroka that I visited early on in my visit to that centre. My role was to encourage the villagers to plant the crop and then gather the fruit and bring it in to the processing centre or sell the fruit to itinerant buyers.

This seemed to work for a while, but the rates at which it was economical to pay for the fruit were low, and it may well be

Pyrethrum

that the local people lost interest. Coffee, for example, or even European potatoes, would have been more lucrative. As far as I know, there is no longer any commercial cropping of passion fruit in Papua New Guinea. There may well, however, be some of the 'Cottees' purple variety displayed at the fresh food markets, along with the yellow variety that grows wild readily and is available for tasting along the village byways.

Pyrethrum

Pyrethrum was another of the number of crops introduced to Papua New Guinea in an attempt to provide income for the villagers. It produces a daisy-like flower that is used to make insecticides. Just about any rapid-acting spray or aerosol bought in stores or pharmacies, in Australia, even today, will contain on its label a reference to a pyrethroid derivative. The active ingredient has the fortunate quality of being lethal to insects but harmless to humans and other mammals. It also breaks down quickly in sunlight, leaving no residues. The relevant issue in this case was the climate. Although Papua New Guinea is well within the band of the tropics, the altitude of the highlands made it possible to establish crops that thrived in cooler conditions but with tropical daylight scenarios. Irish potatoes and Arabica coffee are other examples of these.

With pyrethrum, the altitude is particularly critical when it comes to planting the crop as a viable enterprise. Pyrethrum thrives at very high altitudes in the Papua New Guinea Highlands, with flower production and active constituent content rising steeply the higher up you go. Thus, it was very relevant to the agricultural region I was committed to. The plant was first introduced to Papua New Guinea in 1938. With the push for indigenous income-earning indigenous agricultural development, a thrust was given to its introduction and expansion to the highlands at the time I was stationed there. The crop had been established in Kenya for some time, and in 1957, a selection of planting material was brought for the *didiman* to experiment with.

It has had a fitful history since then and never really been a major source of income. Where it may shine was at the upper levels of habitation of the highlands provinces. It thus may have some value because of the limitations of other potential cash crops.

CHAPTER TWELVE
Health and Census

Census and Yaws Elimination Campaign
Ian Burnett, *kiap;* Harry Jeffries, Medical Assistant (*lik lik dokta*).
Roadhead to tracks to villages, accompanied by police and local medical staff.

Census and Medical Patrol

The monitoring and provision of advice on agricultural matters was not the only government service provided by the Australian administrating authority (officially labelled as the 'Administration' at this stage of Papua New Guinea history). General administration and 'law and order' – the key and very wide-ranging responsibility – was placed with the 'District Officers' and their subordinates the patrol officers. The patrol officers, as *kiaps*, were always present in every established centre. In many cases, they were the only government representatives (often with wives and sometimes families) residing in a given administrative location.

Next would come the medical officers, recognised as *lik lik dokta* in pidgin. Where there were no hospitals or doctors – that applied to just about every village – these medical assistants would inspect the grass-thatched medical centres in the villages and provide whatever health services they and their Papua New Guinean assistants could use considering the limited facilities and supplies.

The Agricultural Officer – *didiman* – thus made up a third arm of a triangle of government services to the village communities.

Occasionally, as can be seen recorded in the above picture, the three agencies found it convenient to have a combined operation. This was the final major expedition of my two-year term in the highlands. Ian Burnett was the resident patrol officer at Lufa and happened to have been the son of Sir Macfarlane Burnett, an Australia winner of the Nobel Prize. A medical institute established in Melbourne continues his contribution to medical research.

Ian and Harry for company:

Monday, 18 February 1957

It has been a very pleasant patrol so far, particularly as Ian and Harry are such good companions. They have none of the idiosyncrasies that can make a person's constant company irritating no matter how much you really like him. Most of our spare time has been spent talking or reading books. There has been none of the card games or draughts we were going to play.

Health, Cannibalism and Kuru

I was talking to someone I met who had been a government officer administering one of the populated areas to the south-east of where my coffee growers operated.[8] It may have been Ludi Schmidt who had taken up a parcel of land east of Goroka. More likely, it was Ian Burnett, the *kiap* you saw being carried across a stream by one of his police officers. He related that in one of the villages he had visited, he had been shown the leg of a deceased young man that was being prepared to be eaten.

Cannibalism in the past in parts of Papua New Guinea is well documented. The killing and eating of missionaries James Chalmers and Oliver Tomkins on 8 April 1901 on Goaribari Island in the Gulf of Papua gained international notoriety. It is claimed that the Korowai tribe not far away in Indonesian Irian Jaya still practises ritual funeral cannibalism.

The cannibalism of the Fore people not far from where I patrolled, however, had a very unfortunate outcome. In their case, this practice was not for hunger satisfaction or revenge on their enemies but as a means of honouring and acquiring the spirit of the dead. Although the Okapa sub-district, home of the Fore people, was not included in my patrol area, they were not far away. Intense research was going on into the deaths, which reached a peak, I learned later, during the decade in which I walked the mountains and valleys of that district.

What apparently happened was that certain changes occurred in the brains of people – certain proteins doubled up to form 'prions.' When the brain tissue of the dead people was fed to living people, these changes grew and caused severe damage to brain functioning. External symptoms included tremor (the word *kuru*

---

[8] Cannibalism: When People Ate People, A Strange Disease Emerged: The Salt: NPR.

from pidgin *guria* – *trembling* and by extension 'earthquake' refers to shaking), and it also became known as the 'laughing' disease. It was always fatal. Research led to establishment of the cause. At one stage, in a population of 1800, 200 people were dying each year. The final death, however, occurred in 2009.

Significantly, however, research on Kuru led to the recognition of what became known as Creuzfeldt-Jakob disease. For people outside Papua New Guinea, the best know example of this malady would be Mad Cow Disease that bedevilled the British beef cattle industry later in the century. In recent years, since those infected at childhood have died and the ritual cannibalism has ceased, there have been no more infections or deaths.

Leprosy and Yaws

Leprosy[9] and yaws were two 'third-world' diseases that were common in Papua New Guinea, including the Highlands. Leprosy

---

[9] At the start of the 21st century, Papua New Guinea declared that leprosy was eliminated.

Remote villages in Papua New Guinea are hard to reach with medical help.

Eliminated – but not eradicated. With the rate dropping below the World Health Organization's elimination threshold – one in ten thousand – the nation's government redirected scarce health money elsewhere.

But leprosy never went away. Eighteen years later, leprosy is back with a vengeance in Australia's nearest neighbour.

The dreaded bacterial disease can take years – or decades – to incubate, with steadily worsening disability from nerve damage, such as a hand frozen, into an unusable claw.

But the historic scourge is now readily treatable with antibiotics, with excellent outcomes if treated early.

Retired GP Dr Colin Martin is the chair of the Leprosy Mission Australia.

'Leprosy never went away in PNG. It's a complicated place, with all these valleys with poor access,' he told *newsGP*.

is apparently making something of a comeback after thought being near eliminated at the end of the last century. Yaws has also had some resurgence in parts of the country. One area of infection, somewhat surprisingly, given the availability of medical services, is in the villages surrounding the capital Port Moresby.

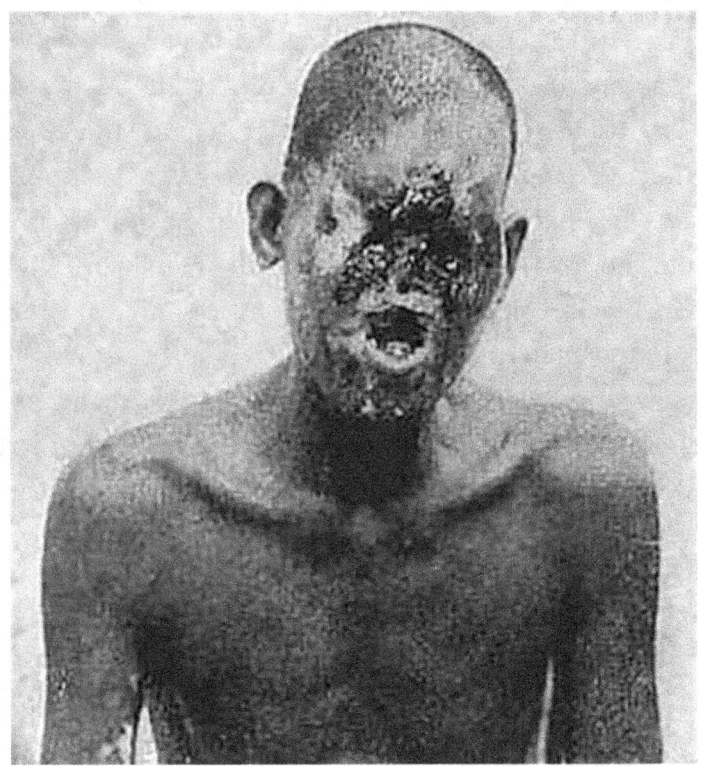

Gangosa – Late Stage of Yaws
Photo - Internet

Yaws is a terribly disfiguring disease, and I observed cases, at first hand in a number of the villages, as bad as that illustrated here (picture not from Papua New Guinea). The purpose of this combined patrol, described here, was a step in a campaign to vaccinate the villagers against yaws.

Yaws was a significant health problem in Papua New Guinea until the nationwide total mass treatment campaign, which took place from 1953 to 1958. The number of cases reported fell to 300 during the 1960s. In the early 1970s, outbreaks occurred in East New Britain and Bougainville but were effectively controlled. A larger outbreak in 1977–1978 on Karkar Island was more difficult to bring under control despite the clinical appearance of the cases, which were less florid than those seen in the 1950s. The latter outbreak raised questions about decreased response to penicillin, lack of ability to develop effective immunity and increased susceptibility to yaws. Smaller outbreaks were reported in 1983 and 1984 in remote areas, but the current extent of yaws in Papua New Guinea is not fully known. Action is being taken to rectify this situation and to ensure that reports of yaws are fully investigated.

Gangosa is a destructive ulceration beginning on the soft palate and extending to the hard palate and nasal passages. It can result in major visible mutilation of the face and mouth. The disease, as far as is known, occurs only in certain parts of the tropics, especially in the islands of the Pacific. It is generally regarded as a sequel to yaws.

Brace Yourselves – Yaws Vaccination with Peanut Oil Base

Fortunately, the treatment to counter the organism causing yaws is very effective. It is an injection of the antibiotic penicillin. So, during the patrol, we were to provide penicillin to members of all the villages we visited. In view of the problems we 21st century Australia have with the anti-vaxxers' response to Coronavirus, it says something for the trust the Papua New Guinea people had in the Australian control and management of their homeland in accepting the inoculation. I was certainly aware of no coercion and no resistance. The villagers would all happily line up in queues to receive their dose of the vaccine.

It must have looked as if I wanted to help. Thus, on one occasion, the *lik lik dokta* invited me to give several of the injections, although I suspect that, as one not medically trained, this was probably not appropriate. The procedure of injecting turned out to be not that easy. The fluid medium that contained the antibiotic comprised peanut oil, which was emulsified rather than dissolved, so it required a large needle to deliver the material to the thigh or buttock. I am sure it must have been painful for the recipients, especially the children.

Vaccination Queue – Children's Turn

There occurred during the vaccinating procedure an event of which I am not proud but which had some significance in my education. All the children were queued up for their vaccination. As is my custom, I went over to them say 'Hullo' and perhaps reassure them about the impending procedure. I spoke a greeting to one boy, perhaps five or six years old. To my surprise (all the young children were naked), he reacted by urinating onto the ground. On seeing this, I think some of his mates may have giggled at him. I, of course, was embarrassed and remain somewhat ashamed to this day. What I had forgotten was that in these parts, seeing a 'white' person could be a rare event. Some children may never have seen a government officer until our visit, so although we may not have been quite seen as bogeymen, for many children being spoken to by a European was a big deal and something to be wary of. The learning experience in this for me was that it illustrated something that I had either not been aware or not experienced. I think I may have read about it and heard that it happens – that fear can invoke a spasm of incontinence. This knowledge can then reinforce my hopes not to frighten anyone.

Now for the Children

They breed these little girls tough. Note the bandage on the hand of the medical assistant to relieve the pressure that the injection with this medium required.

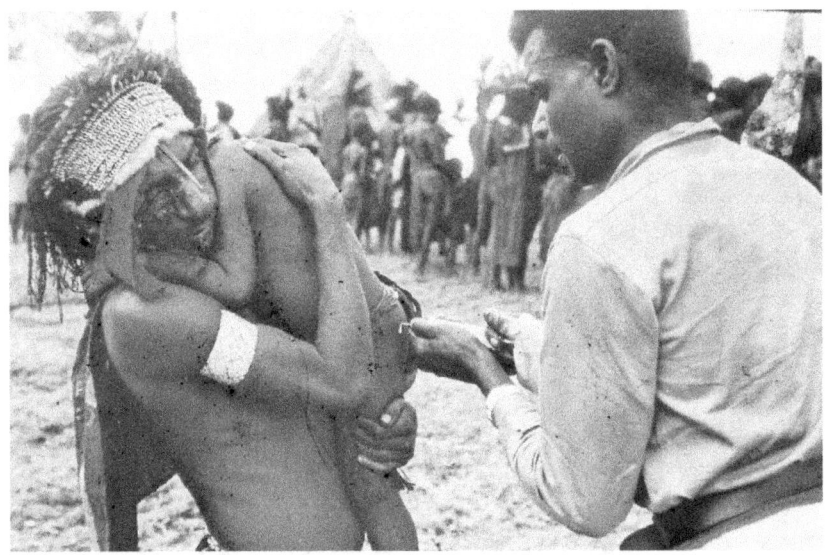

Daddy, It Hurts.
Another example of the children's stoicism

CHAPTER THIRTEEN
Personal Development

Recognition

Life at Goroka was pleasant enough, but I did not have a great deal of social interaction with the European townspeople. Perhaps this gave some impetus to my spending so much time patrolling the villages.

Memory has some strange quirks. In reading my early journals, some of which had not been opened for some 60–70 years, I find the names of individuals of whom I have no recollection at all. As against this, there will be individuals with whom I may have expressed just a sentence or two in a one-off meeting yet find that the words or gestures of that single interaction have stayed in my mind forever. Whether that interaction was good or bad, it is a reminder that our words and actions can have ramifications and effects on other people that we have no way of knowing. In other cases, I found in the journal record a reminder of relationships that were longer and deeper than I recalled. Such was the case with the Goldhardt family.

I have noted my disappointment at not being remembered by Ralph Goldhardt when I met him some 50 years later. My esteem and gratitude for him and his family were renewed recently through a reference in my diary.

Monday, 18 March 1957. I went out to Asaroka after church yesterday to have lunch with and say goodbye finally to the Goldhardts who have always been kind to me in Goroka. Since the Brown-Beresfords, they have been the nearest thing to my own family that I have experienced in this town.

This has happened in other instances of my hopes for a 'claim to fame.' I shared a period as a teacher at the Popondetta Agricultural Training Institute in the late 1960s with Keith De Lacey, who became Queensland State Treasurer and was still a prominent Queensland businessman until he died some time ago. When I approached him at a reunion, some 40 years later, he had no recollection of our shared experiences.

Of course, this may be a common experience with all of us who are not like some 'larger than life' personalities. And it can work the other way.

I was walking down Queen Street in Brisbane one day near the Brisbane GPO, and I heard a voice call out, 'Rodney!'

With some surprise I turned round and this dark-skinned man came up to me and introduced himself. It turned out to be Loa Dou. He had worked with me as one of the clerical staff in the DASF office in Lae. We had not had a close relationship, and yet, he recognised me and sought to get my attention in a crowded city street some 50 years after we had last met and that from some 2,000 kilometres away. Renewal of acquaintances in this way is, I am sure, an experience that many teachers would have.

What leads me to such a reflection in this context, however, is the nearest thing I had to a friendship with a woman while at Goroka.

My immediate boss was Jim Barrie, shown in the photograph earlier. Jim and I did not have a particularly warm relationship. This was my first-ever full-time job, and perhaps in the first raw learning months of employment, there is potential for a few hiccups. Nevertheless, we got on well enough. Rightly or wrongly, I sensed that he saw me as a step below him in the sense that he was a university graduate whereas I was merely the product of a 'farm college.' Once again, rightly or wrongly, perhaps through my own insecurity, this feeling of 'hierarchy' imposed itself on my consciousness when another young man, Ian Sillar, joined our team. Ian was a university graduate, and I gained the impression that because of this, Jim took more notice of Ian than of me. If this were so, it may well have been justified.

I have written earlier of how ill-prepared I was to be an agricultural adviser under Papua New Guinea conditions. This experience may well have had an impact on confirming the inclination, that I already had, to go on to university myself. I subsequently did do that from 1958 to 1962 before returning to Papua New Guinea. On reflection, I feel it was disappointing that when I returned to duty, I was not posted back to my beloved Highlands region.

But this is just leading up to another case of 'recognition' that boosted my spirits.

Jim's wife, Pam, had a new baby, and with this and the strain perhaps of living in this outpost of civilization, she had probably suffered some post-natal depression. So, there were occasions when Jim was away when he may well have asked me to 'keep an eye on her.' Thus, it so happened that I would be invited over for a cup of tea or whatever, and she would converse with me about all things that might be bothering her. So that was that.

It so happened that some 45 years later, I was at a reunion of former Papua New Guinea government officers. My wife, Hazel, was with me, and I think part of the reunion was a trip to Runaway Bay at the Northern end of the Gold Coast.

We were sitting admiring the view and trying to make conversation with people we hardly knew when a middle-aged woman came up to me.

'You don't remember me, do you?'

I had to say, 'No, I'm sorry, I don't.'

She replied, 'I'm Pam, and I used to be Pam Barrie, although Jim and I are divorced now.'

We began to chat about our days at Goroka, and Pam said, 'Do you know why I remember you, Rodney?'

No, tell me,' I said.

Pam replied, 'Well, there was an occasion when I had just been down to the coast and had returned to Goroka in one of the usual DC3 aircraft. My baby had been difficult, and I was feeling harassed about a lot of things. I was by myself and struggling a bit as I came down the aircraft steps. You were waiting there. You saw my difficulty and came up and held the baby for me while I got organised. You were so supportive.'

I had completely forgotten that incident. Perhaps it had never resided in my memory. It was, however, a boost to my sense of hoping to be seen by others, even at the age of 20 years, as the sort of person I wanted to be. Pam's reminiscence has stayed with me ever since.

My action may have started something. In my correspondence from that period, I discovered the following note:

Rodney,

Are you going to the dance tomorrow night? If you aren't, would you like to come to dinner and baby sit for us?

Pam Barrie.

Presumably, I did oblige. What the note confirms is that I did not participate to a large degree in whatever 'social life' was available in the town at that time.

Furthermore, it implies that parents were happy to entrust me with their offspring. One of the lecturers at my agricultural college had in previous years recruited me, a mid-teenage boy, to voluntarily babysit his two young girls. I am comfortable with children (all the more so with my much later involvement as an instructor in Parent Effectiveness Training), despite not having the playful and cuddly personality that some of my later relatives have displayed in their interactions with young ones.

Religious Orientation – Background.

I have referred earlier to the Christian ethical influence that led me to end up in Papua New Guinea.

In opening up recently, for the first time in 67 years, the journal of my three-year's training at Muresk Agricultural College, my eye was caught by the entry of 30 April 1953. One sentence read:

> Mr Coleman, the Government apiculturalist, came up [from headquarters in Perth]. Instead of the usual outdoor inspection, we had an indoor lecture, which I thought was very interesting.'
>
> It is wonderful the ways God has caused the insects to do things almost as if they were human.

It seems from this 'God has caused' that I showed no hesitancy in expressing myself and viewing the world with orthodox Judaeo-Christian terminology. Although I had been educated to junior high school secondary level, I now have no idea whether I had heard of Charles Darwin and the tremendous impact his research and conclusions had on biological and theological study. In my regular association with preaching from the Methodist pulpit, my Sunday school teachers and my boyhood reading, if I had ever heard any suggestion of a non-supernaturalist view of history, it would probably have been referred to in the negative.

Revelation

In the story above about the children going off to sleep on the floor of my room while residing in the village, I noted that I had probably been reading. With so many nights out in the bush with no literate companionship, I had a lot of opportunity to do some serious book reading. To facilitate this, I had an excellent service whereby the public library down in the capital, Port Moresby, could on request make up parcels of books and send them by air on a regular basis to readers scattered throughout the country. You could probably ask them to make up the parcels around specific topics, but I deliberately asked them to send me anything. I saw this as a way of widening my knowledge as well as providing the simple pleasure one could get from reading a good sample of fiction.

It so happened that one book in particular caught my attention and had an effect on my religious perspective that has lasted till this day. It was frustrating to not be able to remember the name of the book, but it had the word 'Jesus' in the title and was written but a man of the Unitarian Christian persuasion. In setting out to write this record of my experiences at that time, however, I discovered that the title of the book had been recorded in my journal at the time. As a result of this discovery, I ordered a second-hand copy of the book from the United States and may get around to re-reading it one day. The book's title is 'Why Jesus Died,' and the author Pierre Van Paassen.

Some 50 more years later, I became very familiar with this writer's exploration of Christian faith. I read John Robinson's 'Honest to God' and Don Cupitt's 'Sea of Faith.' Indeed, I have become something of a proponent of what is now termed 'progressive' Christianity.

I had no idea at that time of what the Unitarian denomination was on about. Anyway, this book presented a picture of Jesus in non-supernatural terms.

My early Christian background, which till then had a major influence on my world view and day-to-day behaviour, had been through the Presbyterian, Methodist and Congregational denominations (in 1977 to combine to form the Uniting Church in Australia). My family's association with a church congregation had provided its main social interaction. My Christian experience, in contrast to so many, had always been benign. The sense of purpose and of community outweighed some of the restrictive doctrines and practices which some found inhibiting. For me, they were absorbed into my psyche that even now, I occasionally sense some uneasiness at partaking of alcohol or playing sport on a Sunday. I remember once asking my young female high school teacher why it was that some people would restrict ballroom dancing.

The idea of a theistic God 'out there' who would do what we wanted if we asked was not something that I placed any dependence on. Nevertheless, I just went with the flow in assuming that a supernatural entity described as 'God' could be a reality. And, of course, the doctrine of the Trinity, developed by the early church long after Jesus had been killed, was something I just went along with. This did not affect the key message of love for one another, even our enemies, which I saw and seek to practice as the heart of the Christian message.

Van Paasen's book, however, showed me that one could have the Jesus story and ethic without its supernatural baggage. From that point on, while lying in those bamboo-walled and grass-thatched residences, I resolved not to base my beliefs and my life on anything that did not match my knowledge and experience of life. That policy has continued for these past 67 years. In that sense, however, I have remained as firmly Christian as ever.

There was something of a sequel to this. At one point during my placement back in Papua New Guinea, during the Western Australian university break, DASF required me to fly to Rabaul on

New Britain, a large island in the east of the country, for a training session or a staff conference. Or it may have been for an interview relating to my application for a university cadetship. While I was at Rabaul, I had the opportunity to attend church services of my own Methodist denomination. Rabaul had a thriving congregation, mainly of people of Chinese descent, including a well-supported group of young people. They made me welcome in their social activities and at one point invited me to attend a small study group. Their minister was an Australian, Rev Ian Fardon, who led the study. Full of enthusiasm over my new perspective from reading the Unitarian book during my highlands patrolling, I raised the possibility that Jesus was a remarkable but otherwise ordinary human being rather than some supernaturally divine person.

The response from Rev Fardon was short and sharp.

'Don't talk rubbish!' he said.

That quickly put me in my place. I shut up then. Those three words have, however, remained with me ever since. Contrarily, they have impelled me to encourage people I associate with, indeed to 'talk rubbish,' if it provides them with a revelation which nurtures their adapting their Christian faith to a 20th or 21st century world.

CHAPTER FOURTEEN
Supplementary Notes

MELANESIAN PIDGIN

Tok Pisin as Lingua Franca

Melanesian pidgin, as practised in Papua New Guinea, is a very interesting language. For the casual observer, with its many derivations, it may appear at first acquaintance as merely broken English. That is not the case. It has a very specific grammar – Francis Mihalic's Grammar and Dictionary of 1957 comprises 318 pages of vocabulary and information.

Although the vocabulary is mainly derived from English words, there are some from other languages. Pronunciation may well vary with the speaker's native language, but in its written form, it is very phonetic, and the vowel sounds closely resemble those of spoken German as far as I can tell.

It also has some traps and misleading expressions that can confuse the speaker of English if this is her or his base language.

Some words might be considered crude, misogynist or denigrating of individuals. It is possible that in the early relationships between European and Melanesian islanders, there were elements of racial differentiation, but as the language developed, its nature as a creole form of communication for contrasting language groups became firmer. It developed terms and phrases which had their own unique meanings not necessarily restricted to the original base expressions.

Some examples:

As: (arse): The biological term of buttock or anus has been extended to mean the foundation or lowest part of something. So, one can say, '*Got, em i as bilong ol.*' The meaning of this is: 'God is the foundation of everything.'

Stap: In English, we use the word 'stop' in two different senses. If we have a guest, we can say, 'She stops with us,' meaning that the person lives at our place. But one can also say, 'The bus stops at the terminus,' meaning that it route ends there and does not go any further. In *tok pisin*, these two meanings can be confused. *Stap* in pidgin employs the first meaning. It means to 'stay,' so, if it is still raining, one might say, '*Ren, em i stap (yet)*. In other words, the rain has not yet finished. The *yet* may be added for emphasis.

Yumi and mipela: Pidgin makes a very useful distinction which, for all the variation and fine tuning of meaning in English, we do not have. In English, when we are addressing a person in a group, 'Let us go fishing,' we make no difference between the suggestion that it is everybody in the group who goes fishing, or only the one person we are talking to goes fishing alone with me. In *tok pisin,* if you are addressing just the one person plus yourself, for 'we,' you use the term *yumi*. If it is the whole group, excluding the person spoken to, however, for 'we,' you use the term *mipela*.

Meri: A newly appointed Administrator of Papua New Guinea before independence in 1975 created a bit of a stir when, after hearing a smattering of pidgin, he got the impression that some of the terms were derogatory or misogynist, so he decreed that Papua New Guinea women were no longer to be referred to as *meri*. This brought protest, because *meri* was the general term used very widely by Papua New Guineans themselves to differentiate female from male (*man*). Similarly the racial distinction, without any implication of relative superiority for Europeans, was displayed by the terms *misis* for European woman and *masta* for European man. It may be that 68 years later, with far more Papua New Guineans conversant in English, that there is more fluidity in these terms. The pidgin plural for 'people' is *manmeri* and for Europeans '*mastamisis.*'

Didiman: This was a term applied to an agricultural extension officer or agricultural research establishment and it led to a distinctiveness and perhaps status in the pidgin language, which was shared by few government authorities other than the patrol officer as *kiap* (perhaps derived from 'captain.') The origin of the term *didiman* is not clear, but the latest consensus seems to be that it was derived from the surname of a German surveyor named Dietman who laid out the original Rabaul Botanical Gardens during the German administration. The term *didimisis* was used later. There was an occasional woman specialist, but there were no female agricultural extension officers until Margaret Mason joined me at Lae in the mid-1960s. It may be noted here that there is no form of the plural for nouns in *tok pisin*, so *didiman* may be either singular or plural. For a number of people, one would add numeric markers such as:

Olgera meri: All the women
Tupela didiman: Two agricultural advisers.
Sampela pig: Some pigs.

Pidgin Phonetics

I found vowels sounded comparably with those used in the German language.

Some examples:

au ow, as in cow or how.
ai i, as in high
u   oo, as in good
a   as, in ah
o   as, in pause
e   as, in pen
i   as, in see

Terminology

Further to the comment on the use of pidgin terms mention might be made of the references differentiating people in this book...

'Papua New Guineans' is used to specify the indigenous inhabitants of the eastern half of the island labelled on maps as New Guinea. That eastern part comprised in roughly equal area the Australian territory of Papua and the United Nations Trust Territory of New Guinea. On 16 September 1975, these two territories were united to form the Independent State of Papua New Guinea.

It is interesting to see how popular language can change significantly. In commenting in the paragraph above on terms used of the local people, now in 2023 the label 'Papua New Guinean' rolled without conscious effort from my mind to the keyboard and paper. On referring back to my diaries, however, I find that the term used freely in 1955 was 'native.' The connotation basically is values-free as referring to someone associated with a particular location – for example, a native of Scotland or a native of Sydney. Somehow, however, when the word is used to denote an indigenous person, that is, originating or occurring naturally in a particular place, 'native' has developed a pejorative tone. People steer away from it and use 'indigenous,' which means just the same thing.

There is another reason, presumably, why I used the word 'native' so freely in my writing in 1955, but now, without being conscious of the difference, slip automatically into Papua New Guinean. It is because the people of that country had not at that time developed a national identity. Papua and the Trust Territory of New Guinea had been administered as two separate political entities, and there was little travel and communication between villagers from one end of the country to another.

There were some fairly large groups sharing identity, but the recorded observation is of 850 different languages in Papua New Guinea for a population of some two million. This indicates how small and narrow must have been the majority of those language groups.

By 1975, however, the people of the two territories came together, forming a combined independent nation with administration centred in Port Moresby. The distinctions, for instance, between Papua and New Guinea which in the past had occasionally been highlighted, dissipated and it became just a matter of fact for the inhabitants to take pride in their now common identity as Papua New Guineans.

It is the Eastern Highlands Province (formerly District) where my tale mainly takes place, they had only been accessible to the world outside their valleys for some 20 years. Living as they did predominantly in their separate residential small pockets of land, it seems appropriate to label the people outside of the town of Goroka, with whom I had most dealings, as 'villagers.'

Non-Papua New Guinea residents may be referred to depending on their roles. Those dealing with the Government and its functions as well as commercial interests (whether or not they were formally Australian citizens) will be noted as Australians. On the other hand, where the context is the culture represented by the Australians, they and those of other nationalities who happened to be present will be described as European and not coming specifically from the continent of Europe. The main purpose of this device will be to distinguish between local culture and introduced culture. It also sometimes serves the purpose of distinguishing between light-skinned and dark-skinned people.

Masta and *misis:* English-speakers on hearing the term in pidgin '*masta*' derived clearly originally from the English word 'master' will link it, as it may well have originally been, to a subservient relationship between a black person and a white person. As pidgin developed, however, this was not the case. '*Masta*' became simply the word in the language for 'European male.' Similarly, '*misis*' became simply the word in the language for 'European female.' In current dictionaries, with so many English language-speakers in the populace, a tendency these days to Anglicise the language and sensitivity to charges of racism, you may find use of '*waitman*' (white man). '*Masta*' was always the word used, unapologetically, in conversations by Papua New Guineans with whom I met. That it was culture rather than skin colour that was significant here is suggested by the use during the war of *blakpela-waitman* for African-Americans by some of the local people.

I don't think there has been any shift from '*misis*.' Note, however, the references above to the challenge to the word '*meri*' as the pidgin word for woman.

References

Bourke, R.M. & Harwod, T. – *Food and Agriculture in Papua New Guinea*. The Australian National University Press, Canberra, 2009.

Dimond, Jarod. – *Collapse – How Societies Choose to Fail or Succeed*. Penguin Books, London, 2006. Chapter 9 – The New Guinea Highlands. In a comprehensive study of how, over thousands of years, human societies have flourished and then collapsed mainly because of failure to recognise the limitations of their natural environment, Jared Dimond highlights, approvingly, the Papua New Guinea Highlands as one of those rare communities, worldwide, which have succeeded in maintaining a sustainable culture.

Godbold, Kim – *The Didiman: The Colonial History of the Australian Agricultural Extension Officers in the Territory of Papua New Guinea, 1945–1975*. 2005. A research paper of the Queensland University of Technology, Carseldine campus, August 2005. Kim Godbold was the daughter of Jack Lamrock, Rodney Eivers's superior in the Department of Agriculture, Stock and Fisheries.

'*Walk into Paradise*'. A feature film. American Cinematographer (1956): Free Download, Borrow, and Streaming: Internet Archive: https://en.wikipedia.org/wiki/Walk_Into_Paradise

www.ingramcontent.com/pod-product-compliance
Lightning Source LLC
Chambersburg PA
CBHW052132110526
44591CB00012B/1689